THE ULTIMATE

CAMPING
ACTIVITY
AND
PUZZLE BOOK

FOR TEENS

MW00934900

CONTAINS HOURS OF FUN CAMPING AND OUTDOOR THEMED PUZZLES AND ACTIVITIES:

Word Searches

Mazes

Would U Rather?

Scavenger Hunts

Trivia

Mad Map Skills

Drawing Prompts

Fallen Phrases

Cryptograms

Crosswords

What To Do When? Survival Skills

Plus...Hangman, Tic Tac Toe,

Rock Paper Scissors, Dots

Copyright © 2023 by River Breeze Press
All rights reserved. This book or any portion thereof
may not be reproduced or used in any manner whatsoever without the express
written permission of the publisher.

THE ULTIMATE CAMPING ACTIVITY & PUZZLE BOOK FOR TEENS

Scavenger Hunt
Around Camp

- [ ] FEATHER
- [ ] FERN
- [ ] LITTER
- [ ] BIKE
- [ ] ROPE
- [ ] MUD
- [ ] ACORN
- [ ] MUSHROOM
- [ ] TRAIL SIGN
- [ ] STARS
- [ ] GRILL
- [ ] LANTERN
- [ ] BUG SPRAY
- [ ] PARK RANGER
- [ ] VINE
- [ ] SAND
- [ ] HOLE IN TREE
- [ ] BERRIES
- [ ] FIREWOOD
- [ ] SUNSCREEN

Puzzle #9 - Campfire Songs

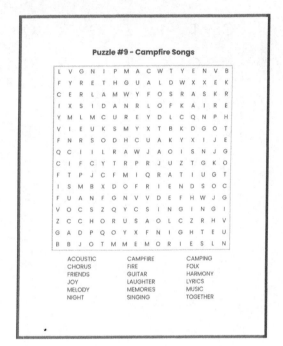

```
L V G N I P M A C W T Y E N V B
F Y R E T H G U A L D W X X E K
C E R L A M W Y F O S R A S K R
I X S I D A N R L O F K A I R E
Y M L M C U R E Y D L C Q N P H
V I E U K S M Y X T B K D G O T
F N R S O D H C U A K Y X I J E
Q C I I L R A W J A O I S N J G
C I F C Y T R P R J U Z T G K O
F T P J C F M I Q R A T I U G T
I S M B X D O F R I E N D S O C
F U A N F G N V V D E F H W J G
V O C S Z Q Y C S I N G I N G I
Z C C H O R U S A O L C Z R H V
G A D P Q O Y X F N I G H T E U
B B J O T M M E M O R I E S L N
```

ACOUSTIC	CAMPFIRE	CAMPING
CHORUS	FIRE	FOLK
FRIENDS	GUITAR	HARMONY
JOY	LAUGHTER	LYRICS
MELODY	MEMORIES	MUSIC
NIGHT	SINGING	TOGETHER

CAMPING ESSENTIALS

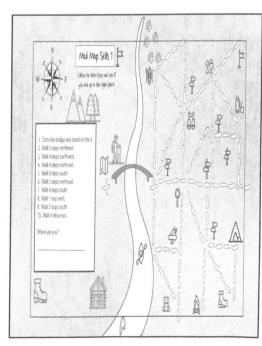

ACROSS

1 Handy for bird watching or scouting the terrain
4 Marked path for hiking or trekking
6 Essential for carrying your gear
8 Provides shelter when camping outdoors
9 Essential for when the weather turns wet
10 Used to cook meals outdoors
15 Handy for seeing in the dark
16 General term for animals living in the natural environment
18 Helps you find your way
19 A bed made of canvas or rope netting, suspended between two trees
20 Used to protect skin from harmful sun rays

DOWN

2 An open-air fire in a camp, used for cooking and as a focal point for social activity
3 Important for dealing with minor injuries
5 Essential to keep the bugs away
7 A sweet treat often roasted over a campfire
11 Paper guide for finding your way around
12 You'll crawl into this for a night under the stars
13 Footwear designed for outdoor walking
14 A popular campfire snack made with graham crackers, chocolate, and marshmallows
17 Used for paddling on the lake

Mad Map Skills 1

Follow the directions and see if you end up in the right place!

1. Cross the bridge and stand on the X
2. Walk 5 steps northwest.
3. Walk 4 steps northwest.
4. Walk 4 steps northeast.
5. Walk 3 steps south.
6. Walk 5 steps northeast.
7. Walk 4 steps south.
8. Walk 1 step west.
9. Walk 3 steps south.
10. Walk 4 steps east.

Where are you?

_____

Puzzle #1 - Haunted Campfire Stories

R	P	L	X	L	K	Q	Q	V	N	O	T	S	T	M	Y
G	T	I	Z	G	K	Q	S	H	Y	K	O	O	P	S	E
N	O	C	T	U	R	N	A	L	C	C	Q	Y	H	R	S
F	T	B	N	K	T	C	Z	F	Y	T	W	Y	Q	Y	S
G	C	D	J	R	R	E	I	R	E	E	I	G	S	C	U
J	Y	Q	H	E	C	S	H	G	L	Z	H	W	R	S	P
O	A	Q	E	M	C	P	M	T	U	O	E	Y	H	W	E
R	B	P	O	A	E	E	S	O	S	H	P	D	A	O	R
G	Y	W	U	E	M	C	A	T	M	T	A	L	U	D	N
Y	F	A	A	R	E	T	T	J	R	S	F	O	N	A	A
Q	O	S	O	C	T	E	N	Q	D	T	A	L	T	H	T
S	L	L	C	S	E	R	A	I	V	A	N	K	E	S	U
U	V	U	N	K	R	A	H	Y	T	B	D	R	D	A	R
X	B	O	D	R	Y	L	P	U	C	K	L	A	J	W	A
S	F	H	J	A	N	M	O	O	N	L	I	G	H	T	L
C	D	G	V	A	A	P	P	A	R	I	T	I	O	N	X

APPARITION   BATS   CEMETERY
CREEPY   CRYPT   EERIE
GHOST   GHOULS   HAUNTED
MOONLIGHT   NOCTURNAL   PHANTASM
SCREAM   SHADOWS   SPECTER
SPOOKY   SUPERNATURAL   WITCH

Maze 1

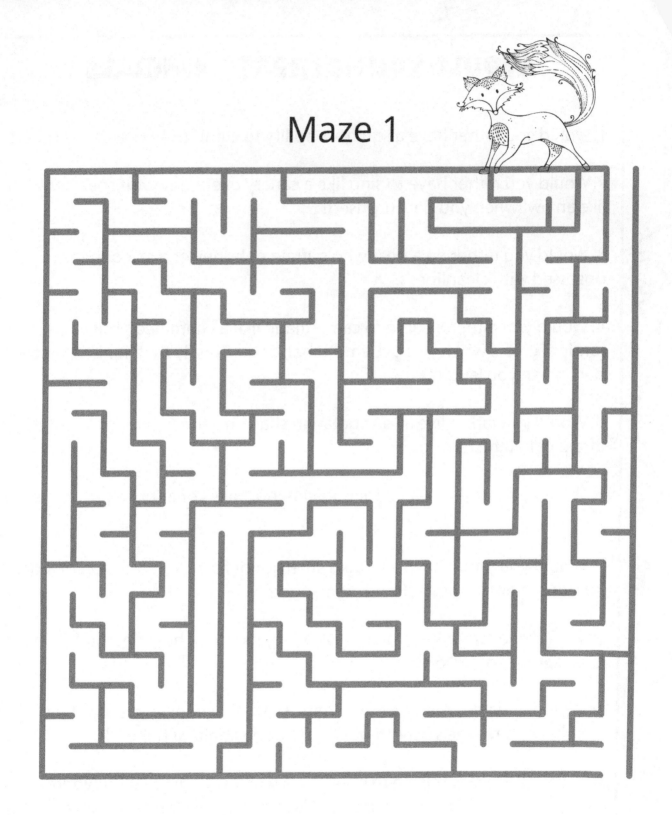

WOULD YOU RATHER? - ANIMALS

1. Would you rather have a squirrel's ability to climb trees or a deer's speed?

2. Would you rather have to sing like a canary every time you speak or hoot like an owl when you get surprised?

3. Would you rather be a bear who's afraid of honey or a raccoon that's obsessed with cleanliness?

4. Would you rather be able to camouflage like a chameleon but change random colors when you get emotional, or be a firefly that lights up in the dark when you laugh?

5. Would you rather live as a vegetarian shark in a forest river or a bird that's afraid of heights?

6. Would you rather be a hedgehog with no spikes or a turtle without a shell?

7. Would you rather have a skunk's smell for defense when scared or a porcupine's quills for protection when angry?

8. Would you rather be a squirrel who forgets where he hides his nuts or a beaver that's afraid of water?

9. Would you rather have the acrobatic skills of a monkey but be afraid of heights or have the strength of a bear but be afraid of the dark?

10. Would you rather have to howl like a wolf every time your favorite song comes on or have to flap your arms like a bird whenever you want to get someone's attention?

WOODLAND WILDLIFE

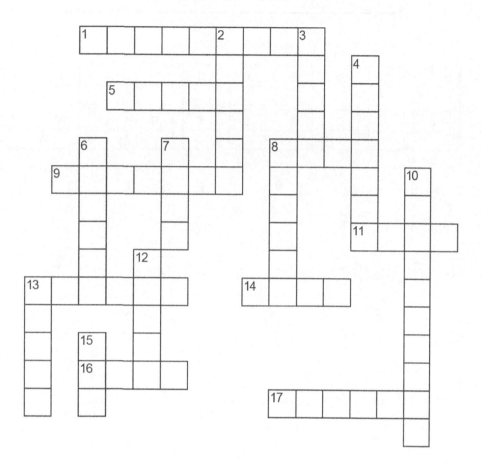

ACROSS

- **1** A rodent known for its coat of spikes
- **5** A large, white, long-necked bird
- **8** A large omnivore found in both North America and Asia
- **9** A mammal known for its masked face and ringed tail
- **11** Canine pack animal, known for its howl
- **13** A predatory insect known for its prayer-like stance
- **14** involving a tadpole stage
- **16** A cat species known for its tufted ears
- **17** A canine native to North America

DOWN

- **2** One of the largest snakes in the world
- **3** Bird of prey known for its keen eyesight and powerful flight)
- **4** A small, often singing bird common in many parts of the world
- **6** A bird of prey known for its speed
- **7** An amphibian with dry, bumpy skin
- **8** A burrowing mammal known for its striking black-and-white face
- **10** An amphibian that can regenerate lost limbs
- **12** The largest mammal in North America
- **13** This large antlered mammal is the tallest species in the deer family
- **15** A large deer species native to North America

CRYPTOGRAM 1

A	B	C	D	E	F	G	H	I	J	K	L	M

N	O	P	Q	R	S	T	U	V	W	X	Y	Z

T _ E _ _ _ _ E S T
H T C Q F K M C U H

_ _ _ _ _ _ _ _ _ _ _ S _
Q G L G D M V K M F D G U B

_ _ _ E _ _ T _ _ _ S _ _ _ _ T
V D C F K H T G U D V H

_ _ _ _ _ E _ _ _ _ E _ _
F Z Q W C A T F Q C V K

_ _ _ E _ E _ _ _ _ T , _ _ _ T
F D C Q C Y T F D H Z W H

_ _ _ S _ _ _ _ _ _ ! _ T _ E
F B W U T K V V B H T C

_ _ _ _ _ _ _ _ _ _
F K B G Q Q F K G F

_ S T _ _ _ _ E _ _ _ E _ S
V U H V I F C J V L C K U

2 , 3 8 4 _ _ _ E S
F J K C U

Scavenger Hunt
Around Camp

- ☐ FEATHER
- ☐ FERN
- ☐ LITTER
- ☐ BIKE
- ☐ ROPE
- ☐ MUD
- ☐ ACORN
- ☐ MUSHROOM
- ☐ TRAIL SIGN
- ☐ STARS

- ☐ GRILL
- ☐ LANTERN
- ☐ BUG SPRAY
- ☐ PARK RANGER
- ☐ VINE
- ☐ SAND
- ☐ HOLE IN TREE
- ☐ BERRIES
- ☐ FIREWOOD
- ☐ SUNSCREEN

FALLEN INSECT FACTS

THE LETTERS OF THESE INTERESTING FACTS ABOUT INSECTS HAVE FALLEN OFF THE BOARD.
LUCKILY THEY LANDED DIRECTLY UNDER WHERE THEY BELONG.

1

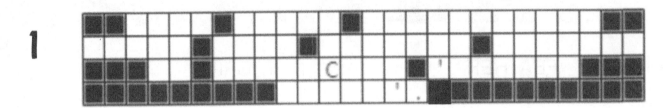

```
            D        I
    E E     O T R A E O U N   O R   T G L O
    B U T   I N H A I N A E R C E S A A T I O N
A B O A N S F S O D R S C T E F   W M G H R E U G H
```

2

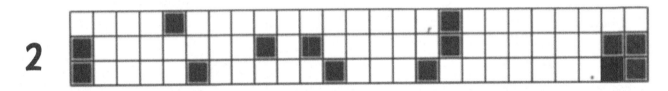

```
F E C     T R   A     N E D       L A Q Y I
S R N R E H E E I T T L E I     O I N U B U
W H E O M T T H E A R E O X G C J L I D T S D G S
```

3

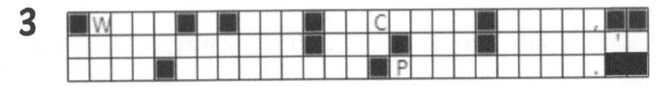

```
    R S G     F   I E T   V R     R H S   W O T S
M O I T O N F L E C S   S U E C T S D   R A R L
D   A T H E A F 9 5 % I A E     E E E A T O R E D   S
```

TRIVIA QUESTIONS

1. Which desert is the driest place on Earth?
   A. Sahara Desert
   B. Atacama Desert
   C. Gobi Desert

2. How many distinct species of trees are in the Amazon Rainforest?
   A. Approximately 5,000
   B. Approximately 16,000
   C. Approximately 40,000

3. Which mountain has the highest vertical rise?
   A. Mount Everest
   B. K2
   C. Denali (Mount McKinley)

4. What is the deepest part of the world's oceans?
   A. Mariana Trench
   B. Puerto Rico Trench
   C. Java Trench

5. What is the most isolated tree on Earth, known as the "loneliest tree in the world"?
   A. Sitka Spruce on Campbell Island
   B. Jomon Sugi in Yakushima Island
   C. Methuselah in White Mountains

6. The North American Pika is not a type of what animal, contrary to its appearance?
   A. Mouse
   B. Rabbit
   C. Squirrel

7. What is the longest cave system in the world?
   A. Mammoth Cave
   B. Lechuguilla Cave
   C. Krubera Cave

8. What is the heaviest bony fish in the world?
   A. Sunfish
   B. Blue Marlin
   C. Swordfish

9. What are the Northern Lights known as in the Southern Hemisphere?
   A. Aurora Australis
   B. Aurora Borealis
   C. Aurora Polaris

Mad Map Skills 1

Follow the directions and see if you end up in the right place!

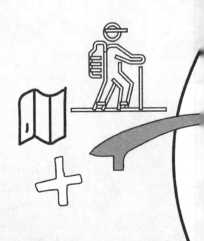

1. Cross the bridge and stand on the X
2. Walk 6 steps northeast.
3. Walk 5 steps south.
4. Walk 4 steps northeast.
5. Walk 4 steps north.
6. Walk 5 steps southeast.
7. Walk 4 steps west.
7. Walk 7 steps south
8. Walk 5 steps southeast.
9. Walk 3 steps north.

Where are you?

_____

Puzzle #2 - Outdoor Activities

```
U K Z H D G N I H C A C O E G O
G A X G N I H S I F L R T R I P
P Y Y Z J N T X G N I M M I W S
N A G E B N G N I Z A G R A T S
U K R N U I A U R V P W B X M R
F I G H I W K R H A E X O H A O
B N S W F K L I C F L M I F C Y
D G O G Z Z L H N H P A T P B X
P E F P Z T Y A E G E I P R V M
Z L E C U P F V W Z N R Y X A L
E L C V G D Z A J G I G Y U G E
C O O K I N G H I K I N G I O Y
K Y O E A H F C L I M B I N G P
Y K W I W N E Q C A N O E I N G
C L I M B I N G T R A C K I N G
B G E G N I N I L P I Z T H C Y
```

ARCHERY	BIKING	CANOEING
CLIMBING	COOKING	FISHING
GEOCACHING	HIKING	HUNT
KAYAKING	RAFTING	STARGAZING
SWIMMING	TRACKING	WALKING
ZIP-LINING		

Maze 2

WOULD U RATHER? - CAMP FOOD

1. Would you rather eat a marshmallow that fell in the dirt or a hot dog that got stuck in a tree?

2. Would you rather cook your dinner over a campfire using a flaming marshmallow as your only utensil or attempt to grill your food using a magnifying glass as a heat source?

3. Would you rather eat a s'more with burnt marshmallows or a burnt pancake with maple syrup?

4. Would you rather drink a cup of lukewarm campfire coffee or a cup of cold, melted ice from the cooler?

5. Would you rather eat a bowl of cereal with powdered milk that's been sitting in your backpack for a week or a bowl of cereal with ants as an added protein?

6. Would you rather have your camping dinner consist of only beans for the entire trip or a can of sardines for every meal?

7. Would you rather accidentally mistake a rock for a potato while cooking or accidentally mistake a stick for a hot dog while roasting it?

8. Would you rather eat a trail mix that's only made up of raisins and pinecones or a trail mix with bugs and worms as surprise ingredients?

9. Would you rather cook your campfire meal using a pot that's been previously used as a bird bath or a frying pan that was mistaken for a frisbee?

10. Would you rather have to catch and cook your own dinner by fishing with a shoe lace or by hunting with a slingshot?

FOREST FLORA

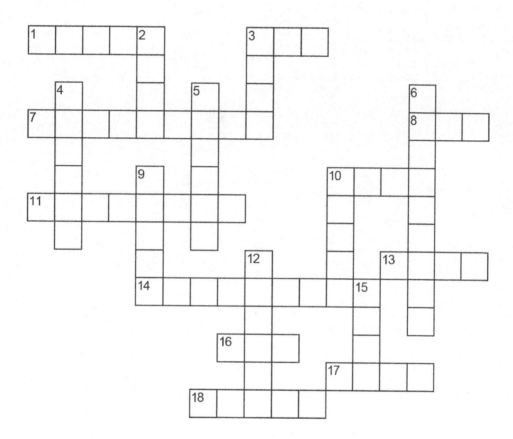

ACROSS

1 This plant, with its brightly colored flowers, is a symbol of Holland
3 A type of evergreen tree often used as a Christmas tree
7 Yellow flower that becomes a puffball of seeds
8 A large tree known for its acorns
10 Soft plant often found on the north side of trees
11 A type of fungus that comes in many varieties, not all of them edible
13 This flowering plant often grows in ponds
14 This tall plant turns to follow the sun
16 Climbing vine often found in forests
17 An unwanted plant in a garden
18 Tree with distinctive white bark

DOWN

2 This evergreen tree has needles instead of leaves
3 Non-flowering plant with feather-like leaves
4 Spiky plant that thrives in desert conditions
5 A tree known for its long, drooping branches
6 Plant known for causing itchy skin rash
9 Covers the ground in most fields and lawns
10 Known for its syrup and distinctive leaf shape
12 This plant is lucky if you find one with four leaves
15 Thorny plant known for its fragrant flowers

CRYPTOGRAM 2

A	B	C	D	E	F	G	H	I	J	K	L	M

N	O	P	Q	R	S	T	U	V	W	X	Y	Z

S _ _ _ _ _ E _ S _ _ _ E
E N V O K K M B E   Q K M

_ _ _ _ E _ _ _ E
O S Z K M G O X B M

_ _ _ _ E _ S _ _ _
Z B O R X M K E   Q S G

_ _ _ _ E _ S . _ T _ E
A V R H M K E   D I M P

_ _ _ _ _ _ _ _ _ T _
Z Q S   A V R H   V H   D U

2 0 _ E E T _ _ _ _ _ _
    W M M D   Q S G   Z Q S

_ _ _ _ _ _ _ _ _
W Q B B   W K U R   Q

_ E _ _ _ T _ _ 1 0 0
I M O Y I D   U W

_ E E T _ _ T _ _ _ T
W M M D   J O D I U V D

_ E T T _ _ _ _ _ _ _ T .
Y M D D O S Y   I V K D

WHAT TO DO WHEN...

Take turns with someone else at camp to see if you know the best way to handle these wilderness survival situations.

- - WHAT TO DO WHEN YOU'RE LOST - -

Stop, Think, Observe, and Plan (STOP). Don't panic or start moving aimlessly. Get your bearings, find a safe spot, and start signaling for help. Create a plan based on your supplies, the environment, and your energy level.

- - WHAT TO DO WHEN YOU ENCOUNTER A WILD ANIMAL - -

Stay calm and do not run. Make yourself appear bigger, make noise, and slowly back away. Every animal behaves differently, so it's important to know how to handle encounters with local wildlife before heading out.

- - WHAT TO DO WHEN YOU RUN OUT OF WATER - -

Begin looking for fresh water immediately. Look for a running stream or river, or collect rainwater if possible. In dire situations, you can even collect morning dew off plants. Always purify water if you can, through boiling or using purification tablets.

- - WHAT TO DO WHEN IT STARTS TO RAIN HEAVILY - -

Seek or build a shelter immediately to stay dry and avoid hypothermia. If you have a tarp or waterproof material, use it. Collect rainwater for drinking if you have a container.

- - WHAT TO DO WHEN YOU INJURE YOURSELF - -

Clean the wound immediately with clean water if available, apply a disinfectant if you have one, and bandage the wound. Seek professional medical help as soon as possible.

4

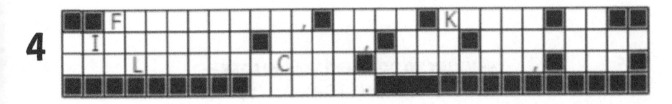

```
              L         S
   O  RMINIFSUNS   O E OC    AL
L GHTEINGSBEGT BERTNAWN ASL
BI IUNFLEE IEALSAE LESTUNOTY
```

5

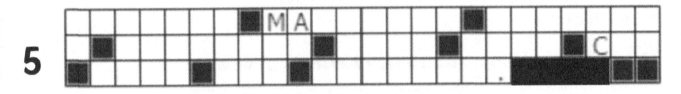

```
      ALN G      NGCE      A
PTFYIX180ENTIRESSP TS AS
ARURENIBL DEESKETHOS ESN
```

6

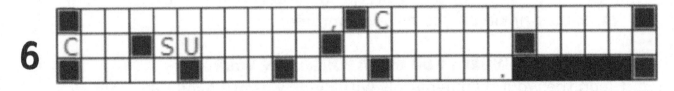

```
  AE    FAR Y     OHOR    C  I
HEAD ROBLE W WEKUO THES
RNMARKVIVONEITCEKTA HE R
```

10. What is the oldest living tree species?
    A. Bristlecone Pine
    B. Olive Tree
    C. Norway Spruce

11. What is the name for a narrow strip of land with sea on either side, forming a link between two larger areas of land?
    A. Isthmus
    B. Peninsula
    C. Cape

12. How many time zones are there in Antarctica?
    A. 24
    B. 12
    C. 1

13. How many moons does the planet Mars have?
    A. 1
    B. 2
    C. 3

14. What is the tallest species of grass?
    A. Wheat
    B. Bamboo
    C. Pampas

15. Which bird can fly backwards?
    A. Sparrow
    B. Hummingbird
    C. Kingfisher

16. What is the highest waterfall in the United States?
    A. Niagara Falls
    B. Yosemite Falls
    C. Multnomah Falls

17. Which insect migrates from Canada to Mexico each year?
    A. Monarch Butterfly
    B. Honey Bee
    C. Canadian Soldier

18. How old is the Great Barrier Reef estimated to be?
    A. 500,000 years old
    B. 1 million years old
    C. 2 million years old

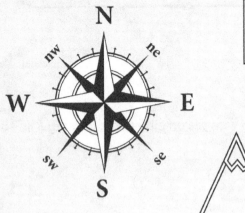

Mad Map Skills 2

Follow the directions and see if you end up in the right place!

1. Cross the bridge and stand on the X
2. Walk 6 steps north.
3. Walk 5 steps southeast.
4. Walk 5 steps south.
5. Walk 5 steps southeast.
6. Walk 4 steps north.
7. Walk 3 steps east.
7. Walk 4 steps north
8. Walk 5 steps northwest.

Where are you?

_____

Puzzle #3 - Campfire Foods

```
I  H  A  M  B  U  R  G  E  R  S  S  E  D  S  R
W  K  S  U  F  D  T  O  S  L  D  A  G  P  Y  W
Y  S  D  K  O  C  S  E  K  A  C  N  A  P  C  Y
X  Z  O  G  C  K  B  N  D  I  Y  P  Y  U  P  V
C  M  S  H  U  I  S  F  Y  N  A  B  X  I  P  E
Q  U  B  C  C  N  T  A  D  C  W  M  Z  T  S  S
U  Y  W  C  V  A  U  S  K  I  S  Z  Z  K  T  I
E  M  V  H  H  E  N  E  D  N  A  E  E  E  S  I
S  P  F  C  Q  A  T  W  D  A  D  W  W  S  B  L
A  O  T  A  C  O  S  R  O  J  E  M  P  M  Q  I
D  T  I  Y  N  F  V  M  T  R  D  R  Q  O  V  H
I  A  N  D  J  C  R  I  S  P  H  A  B  R  R  C
L  T  C  O  R  N  N  J  X  E  N  M  G  E  L  U
L  O  R  O  L  L  S  B  W  U  J  V  P  S  B  X
A  E  P  O  P  C  O  R  N  P  O  G  N  T  S  I
S  S  A  V  E  G  E  T  A  B  L  E  S  T  A  J
```

BREADSTICKS   CHILI   CORN
CRISP   DOGS   HAMBURGERS
NACHOS   PACKET   PANCAKES
PIZZA   POPCORN   POTATOES
QUESADILLAS   ROLLS   SKEWERS
SMORES   STEW   TACOS
VEGETABLES

Maze 3

WOULD U RATHER? - HAUNTED

1. Would you rather spend the night in a forest rumored to be haunted by a headless ghost or in an abandoned cabin said to be visited by a ghostly apparition every night?

2. Would you rather get lost in a dark and foggy forest with no compass or flashlight or have to spend the night alone on a supposedly cursed island?

3. Would you rather hear eerie whispers outside your tent at night or wake up to find strange, unidentifiable footprints around your campsite?

4. Would you rather have your campfire inexplicably go out in the middle of telling ghost stories or hear a distant, creepy laughter in the woods while you're trying to sleep?

5. Would you rather be trapped in the woods during a full moon, with howls echoing in the distance, or in a sudden, unexplainable thunderstorm where your only shelter is a cave that seems to have something moving inside?

6. Would you rather find an old, worn-out doll in the middle of the woods or see a pair of glowing eyes watching you from the darkness?

7. Would you rather have your only flashlight start flickering and then go out while exploring a cave or have your phone ring in the middle of the night, with the caller ID showing an unknown number?

8. Would you rather come across a strange, half-human creature in the forest during the day or hear the rustling of leaves and breaking of twigs just outside your tent all through the night?

9. Would you rather feel something brushing against your foot in a dark lake while swimming or see a figure standing on the edge of the lake when you're the only one supposed to be there?

10. Would you rather find an old, decrepit graveyard near your campsite or stumble upon an abandoned house in the middle of the woods?

CAMPING ESSENTIALS

ACROSS

1 Handy for bird watching or scouting the terrain

4 Marked path for hiking or trekking

6 Essential for carrying your gear

8 Provides shelter when camping outdoors

9 Essential for when the weather turns wet

10 Used to cook meals outdoors

15 Handy for seeing in the dark

16 General term for animals living in the natural environment

18 Helps you find your way

19 A bed made of canvas or rope netting, suspended between two trees

20 Used to protect skin from harmful sun rays

DOWN

2 An open-air fire in a camp, used for cooking and as a focal point for social activity

3 Important for dealing with minor injuries

5 Essential to keep the bugs away

7 A sweet treat often roasted over a campfire

11 Paper guide for finding your way around

12 You'll crawl into this for a night under the stars

13 Footwear designed for outdoor walking

14 A popular campfire snack made with graham crackers, chocolate, and marshmallows

17 Used for paddling on the lake

CRYPTOGRAM 3

A	B	C	D	E	F	G	H	I	J	K	L	M

N	O	P	Q	R	S	T	U	V	W	X	Y	Z

```
_ _ _ _ _ _ _     _ _ _
G O M J V P E     G O P

            _ _E_ _ _ _ _ _
V M J S C H Q   N C U S

S_ _ E_E_ _     _ _ _T_T E_ _ _S_ .
R Y Q Q J   J O X X Q S P R

_ _E_ _ _     _E_ _ _S_E_ _     _T_ _
K Q V P E   Q L J C R Q F   X C

_ _E_T_ _ _     _ _E_ _T_
P O X U S O Y   Y V E A X

_ _ _ _ _ _     T_ _E_     _ _ _
F U S V P E   X A Q   F O N

_ _E_ _S_     _ _E_ _ _ _T_E_
A Q Y J R   S Q E U Y O X Q

_ _ _ _     _ _ _ _ ' S_
N C U S   K C F N   R

_ _T_E_ _ _ _ _     _ _ _ _ _ .
V P X Q S P O Y   G Y C G I
```

DRAWING - LANDSCAPE STORY

Draw the landscape you see from your camping spot. Then, add something fantastical to it - maybe a mythical creature, a hidden door in a hill, a floating island in the sky, or even a UFO.

FALLEN INSECT FACTS

THE LETTERS OF THESE INTERESTING FACTS ABOUT INSECTS HAVE FALLEN OFF THE BOARD.
LUCKILY THEY LANDED DIRECTLY UNDER WHERE THEY BELONG.

7

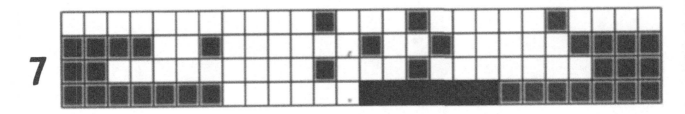

```
    T I E S       A      C
  T O   T H R R   R E   L T E A T
  R E C R F L A S S E A S   S   O A I T E F
B U T T E E P T O E T E U   E   T H   S R E D E E T
```

8

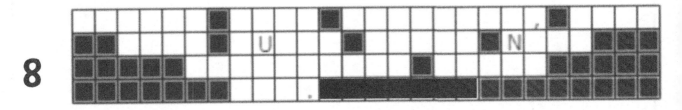

```
    R O U         P O
  R   Q H Y G K   U E E P R
T H E T   D A A C   S L   W E H N I A   S
R A T A K E H T   I N H O   T   T I E G R P A N T S
```

9

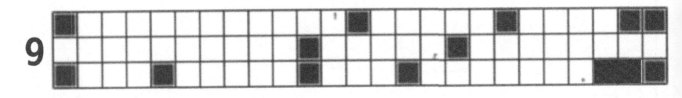

```
  M O R   U E T T E       S     R   N L
N C O Q B I A O S   F A W I N E C O F C A I
I S O S E D I B L Y S P E R T S G S E A D H P N G
```

19. The only sea without any coasts is:
    A. The Red Sea
    B. The Dead Sea
    C. The Sargasso Sea

20. How much of the world's freshwater is stored in glaciers?
    A. 25%
    B. 50%
    C. 69%

21. What is the only mammal capable of sustained flight?
    A. Bat
    B. Flying Squirrel
    C. Colugo

22. What is the smallest species of bird?
    A. Hummingbird
    B. Goldcrest
    C. Kiwi

23. Which mountain range is Mount Everest located in?
    A. The Alps
    B. The Himalayas
    C. The Andes

24. What is the scientific name for the study of trees?
    A. Dendrology
    B. Botany
    C. Arboriculture

25. What is the highest active volcano in the world?
    A. Mount Vesuvius
    B. Mount Etna
    C. Ojos del Salado

26. How long is the Great Wall of China?
    A. 13,170 miles
    B. 5,500 miles
    C. 21,196 miles

27. What is the driest continent on Earth?
    A. Africa
    B. Australia
    C. Antarctica

Mad Map Skills 3

Follow the directions and see if you end up in the right place!

1. Cross the bridge and stand on the X
2. Walk 3 steps south.
3. Paddle north to the dock.
4. Walk 4 steps southeast
5. Walk 5 steps south.
6. Walk 5 steps northeast.
7. Walk 2 steps north.
8. Walk 5 steps southeast.
9. Walk 4 steps west.
10. Walk 6 steps south.
11. Walk 5 steps southeast
12. Walk 3 steps north.

Where are you?

_____

Puzzle #4 - National Parks

```
K Q I A B S G O B A D L A N D S
R Y W N Y K E F L K T T Q R Z F
Q O G H R H D Q Z Y W O O B D T
H S D U R U H K U P M C U T R L
I E F M L V B J I O K P G S J Y
L M L D P B L I Q Y I Y I P O T
A I K B R D A C A D I A U C S E
N T J Y Y E O S N I K E Y U H R
E E C K L V R O O V T P A Q U E
D E O F J E Y A W V W O P G A I
E M A Q F N A E I D S R L D X C
S Y L C A Q V Z I N E N E B T A
G P V C Q H G P I I I R H G H L
T H F A R C H E S O B E G J O G
N T E T O N N G X Y N G R P O Z
X V O B E V E R G L A D E S L E
```

ACADIA	ARCHES	BADLANDS
BRYCE	CANYON	DENALI
EVERGLADES	GLACIER	JOSHUA
OLYMPIC	RAINIER	REDWOOD
ROCKY	SEQUOIA	SMOKY
TETON	YOSEMITE	ZION

Maze 4

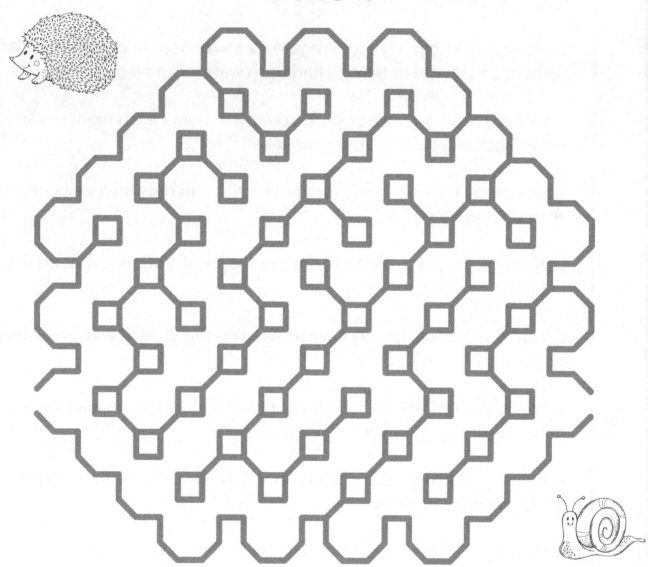

WOULD U RATHER? - SURVIVAL

1. Would you rather have to start a fire without matches or cook all your meals over an open flame?

2. Would you rather have to navigate your way back to camp in the dark without a flashlight or have to find fresh water with no map?

3. Would you rather have to build your own shelter each night or carry a heavy backpack with all your supplies all day?

4. Would you rather eat only foraged berries and nuts for a week or catch and cook your own fish?

5. Would you rather have an unlimited supply of sunscreen but no hat, or a hat but no sunscreen?

6. Would you rather always have to sleep on the ground without a sleeping bag or never have a pillow?

7. Would you rather have a high-quality multi-tool but no manual or a detailed survival guide but no tools?

8. Would you rather deal with a week of non-stop rain or have no water source near your campsite?

9. Would you rather have a camping buddy who's too cautious or one who's recklessly adventurous?

10. Would you rather forget your bug repellent or your first-aid kit?

WILD WEATHER

ACROSS

4 A powerful natural electrostatic discharge produced during a thunderstorm.

6 A cloud of tiny water droplets suspended in the atmosphere at or near the earth's surface that limits visibility.

8 Light rain falling in very fine drops.

9 A prolonged period of abnormally low rainfall.

11 A prolonged period of excessively hot weather, which may be accompanied by high humidity.

13 The sound caused by a lightning discharge.

14 A severe snowstorm with high winds and low visibility.

16 An arch of colors formed in the sky in certain circumstances, caused by the refraction and dispersion of the sun's light by rain.

18 A thick cloud of tiny water droplets suspended in the atmosphere at or near the earth's surface.

20 With a lot of wind.

21 A system of winds rotating inward to an area of low atmospheric pressure.

22 A sudden and violent shaking of the ground as a result of movements within the earth's crust.

23 A windstorm that lifts up clouds of sand or dust.

24 Of, typical of, or peculiar to the tropics.

DOWN

1 An overflow of water that submerges land which is usually dry.

2 The amount of water vapor in the air, often associated with the potential for precipitation.

3 A mass of snow, ice, and rocks falling rapidly down a mountainside.

5 A long high sea wave caused by an earthquake, submarine landslide, or other disturbance.

7 A rotating column of air that can cause significant destruction.

10 Below 32 degrees Fahrenheit (0 degrees Celsius).

11 A storm with a violent wind, in particular a tropical cyclone in the Caribbean.

12 A storm that drops hail, or lumps of ice.

15 A seasonal prevailing wind in the region of South and Southeast Asia, bringing heavy rainfall.

17 A tropical storm in the region of the Indian or western Pacific oceans.

19 A form of precipitation consisting of ice pellets, often mixed with rain or snow.

CRYPTOGRAM 4

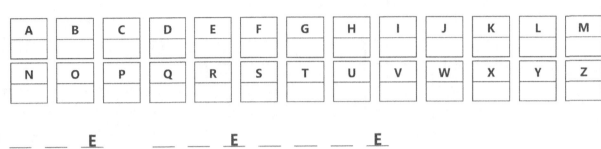

A	B	C	D	E	F	G	H	I	J	K	L	M
N	O	P	Q	R	S	T	U	V	W	X	Y	Z

```
__ __ E__   __ __ E__   __ __ E__
Z  W  B     R  U  B  O  R  H  B

__ __ __ __ __ __ __ __ __ __
W  S  E  E  F  L  H  A  F  O  V

__ E__ __ __ __ S__    __ E__ S__ S__    __ __ __ __
T  B  F  H  W  D       X  B  D  D        Z  W  R  L

__    __ __ __ __ E__ __    __ __ __    __ __ S__
R     L  F  P  C  B  X      A  S  Z     W  R  D

__    __ E__ __ __ __    __ __ __ __
R     W  B  R  O  Z      Z  W  R  Z

__ E__ __ __ S__    __ __    __ __
A  B  R  Z  D       S  N     Z  K

1 , 2 6 0    __ __ __ E__ S__    __ __ E__
             Z  F  E  B  D        N  B  O

__ __ __ __ E__ .
E  F  L  S  Z  B
```

Scavenger Hunt- Leaves

Find 8 different shaped LEAVES Draw them below

DON'T TOUCH THE LEAVES - THEY COULD BE POISONOUS!

THE LETTERS OF THESE INTERESTING FACTS ABOUT INSECTS HAVE FALLEN OFF THE BOARD.
LUCKILY THEY LANDED DIRECTLY UNDER WHERE THEY BELONG.

10

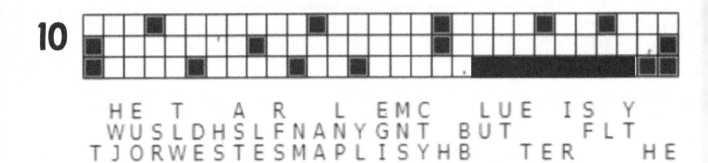

```
HE T   A R   L EMC   LUE  IS Y
WUSLDHSLFNANYGNT BUT    FLT
TJORWESTESMAPLISYHB  TER    HE
```

11

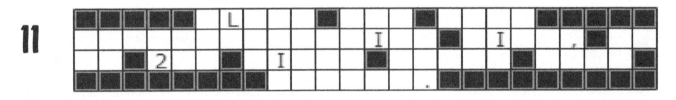

```
        E  G  L
    O  DINNSTN    H
EO     OF  TASAR  HYEIMGB      U
TXTRAORELMECATHJURPHODYP
```

12

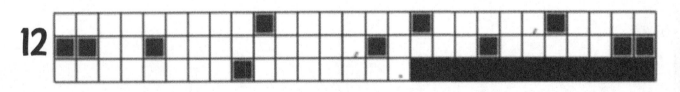

```
  LK  AEX   CEE        SM        I
SALNWORMTILANDTFR  I  K     US D
SIIIVTRYSGLRSASE  O  LTHE  RE
```

28. What is the longest continental mountain range in the world?
    A. The Himalayas
    B. The Andes
    C. The Rockies

29. Which country has the most lakes in the world?
    A. United States
    B. Canada
    C. Russia

30. What is the national bird of New Zealand?
    A. Emu
    B. Kiwi
    C. Kookaburra

31. Which bird is known for its elaborate courtship dance?
    A. Peacock
    B. Bowerbird
    C. Bird of Paradise

32. Which country does the island of Borneo belong to?
    A. Malaysia and Indonesia
    B. Philippines
    C. Australia

33. Which planet in our solar system has the most moons?
    A. Jupiter
    B. Saturn
    C. Uranus

34. What is the name of the supercontinent that existed approximately 200 million years ago?
    A. Pangea
    B. Gondwana
    C. Laurasia

35. What is the highest possible score in a standard game of 18-hole disc golf?
    A. 36
    B. 54
    C. 72

36. Which is the largest species of penguin?
    A. Emperor Penguin
    B. King Penguin
    C. Adélie Penguin

Mad Map Skills 4

Follow the directions and see if you end up in the right place!

1. Cross the bridge and stand on the X
2. Walk 7 steps north.
3. Paddle south to the dock.
4. Walk 4 steps east.
5. Walk 4 steps north.
6. Walk 7 steps east.
7. Walk 3 steps north.
8. Walk 5 steps northwest.
9. Walk 3 steps south.
10. Walk 5 steps southwest.
11. Walk 4 steps west.

Where are you?

_____

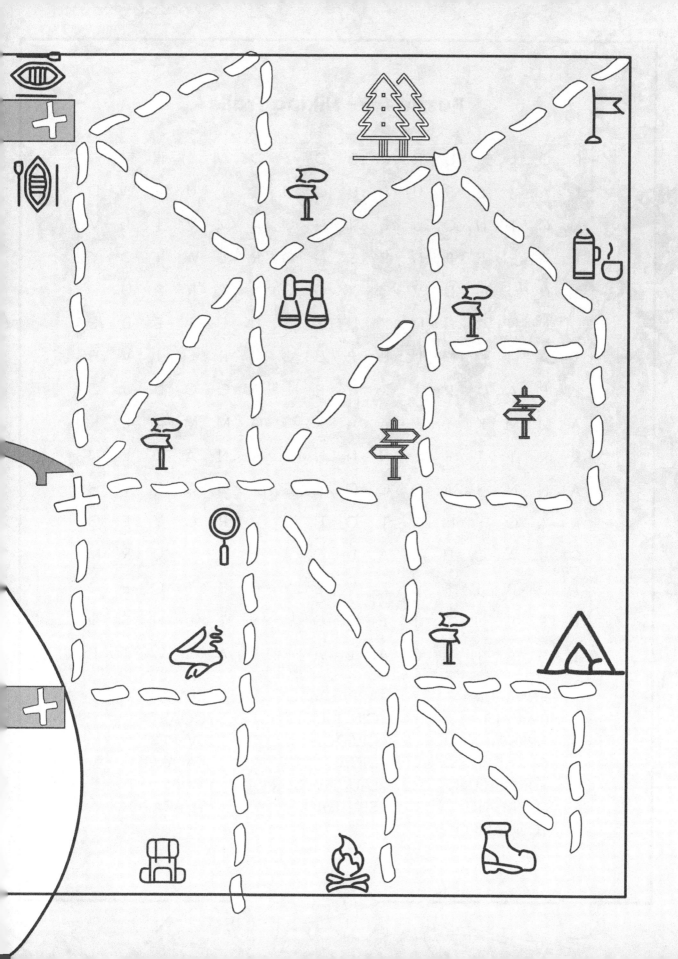

Puzzle #5 - Hiking Trails

```
P O L I U R K B D Z D W L N M W
L A Z E S U W U O N Q I U J W D
X C I N Q U E J N Q A M V T L V
L A R E P D P G N G R L W I O Y
I N U F D V Q X Q G S T R R D P
D N N C H M X U T J U L I E B E
T A C M M U B P B G Q R E I V H
E P A A R I K K R L A O G D J O
A U M K T R A A X G A M M N E K
R R I T F L N N S R N A D E N
A N N J A D C O A S T C C Q V H
R A O L M X T O H Z V R C Y E O
O J A Q U L A U G A V E G U R M
A U B J E D F V E Y N S T C E C
P S E N T I E R O W N T L H S D
L N A I H C A L A P P A S W T F
```

ANNAPURNA   APPALACHIAN   BLANC
CAMINO   CINQUE   COAST
CREST   DIVIDE   EVEREST
GRAND   INCA   KALALAU
KUNGSLEDEN   LAUGAVEGUR   MUIR
OVERLAND   SENTIERO   TE ARAROA
TONGARIRO

Maze 5

WOULD U RATHER? - NATURE

1. Would you rather be able to talk to animals or have plants grow wherever you touch the ground?

2. Would you rather sleep under a waterfall or in a treehouse?

3. Would you rather have the ability to breathe underwater and explore a lake or be able to fly and skim the tops of the trees?

4. Would you rather see a meteor shower or a rainbow every day at camp?

5. Would you rather camp in a place with no nightfall or a place with no daylight?

6. Would you rather witness a volcanic eruption from a safe distance or experience an earthquake that didn't cause any damage?

7. Would you rather have the lake turn into a giant hot tub when you enter or have every rock become a soft pillow when you sit on it?

8. Would you rather swim with friendly dolphins in a crystal clear sea or stroll with a herd of deer in a tranquil forest?

9. Would you rather be able to climb any mountain effortlessly or be able to walk across any body of water?

10. Would you rather experience a forest with trees that change colors every day or a sky that changes colors every hour?

BIRDS OF A FEATHER

ACROSS

2 Large waterbird with a long flexible neck, short legs, webbed feet, a broad bill, and typically all-white plumage

3 A bird of the pigeon family Columbidae, known for their cooing sound

9 Small bird that can be found in most parts of the world

10 Large bird of prey with a massive hooked bill, white head and long, broad wings

13 A bird of prey with long pointed wings and a notched beak, typically catching prey by diving on it from above

14 A bird with a hard chisel-like bill for boring into wood for insects

16 Large water bird characterized by a long beak and a large throat pouch used for catching prey

17 A bird known for carrying messages

18 Seed-eating songbird that typically has a stout bill and colorful plumage

19 A small insectivorous passerine bird that was formerly classed as a member of the thrush family

DOWN

1 The most common North American bird known for it's bright red coloring.

4 Large, black bird, known for its intelligence and presence in many cultural mythologies

5 A small nectar-feeding bird, characterized by its ability to hover and fast wing-flapping rates

6 It is the largest living bird.

7 Nocturnal bird of prey with large forward-facing eyes

8 Often colorful bird, known for its ability to mimic human speech

11 A bird native to North America, recognizable by its blue body and crest on its head

12 Flightless bird living mostly in the Southern Hemisphere, especially in Antarctica.

13 Wading bird known for its distinctive pink color

15 Has very long tail feathers that have eye-like markings.

CRYPTOGRAM 5

A	B	C	D	E	F	G	H	I	J	K	L	M

N	O	P	Q	R	S	T	U	V	W	X	Y	Z

T _ _   A _ _ A _ A _ _ _ A _
N E O   T L L T K T I E C T M

T _ A _ _ ,   _ T _ _ _ T _ _ _
N P T C K   V N P O N I E O V

_ _ _ _   2 , 1 9 0   _ _ _ _
F W O P   X C K O V

(3 , 5 2 4

_ _ _ _ _ _ T _ _ _)   _ _ _ _
Z C K F X O N O P V   A P F X

_ _ _ _ _ _ A _ T _ _
H O F P H C T N F

_ A _ _ _ ,   _ A _ _ _ _ _
X T C M O   L T V V C M H

T _ _ _ _ _ _ _ _ _ _ T _ _ _
N E P F J H E A F J P N O O M

_ _ T A T _ _ .
V N T N O V

WHAT TO DO WHEN...

Take turns with someone else at camp to see if you know the best way to handle these wilderness survival situations.

- - WHAT TO DO WHEN YOU ENCOUNTER POISONOUS PLANTS OR INSECTS - -

If you've touched a poisonous plant, rinse the area with water and soap if possible, and avoid touching your face or eyes. For insect bites, clean the area, apply a cool compress, and monitor for any unusual reactions.

- - WHAT TO DO WHEN YOUR FIRE WON'T LIGHT - -

Ensure that your tinder is dry and that you have enough kindling to sustain a flame once it starts. If all of your materials are wet, try finding drier material under large trees or rocks, or inside dead standing trees.

- - WHAT TO DO WHEN YOU'RE RUNNING OUT OF FOOD - -

Look for edible plants, but be certain they're safe to eat. Small animals, insects, and fish can be a source of protein.

- - WHAT TO DO WHEN IT GETS EXTREMELY COLD - -

Keep moving to generate body heat, but don't sweat as this can freeze and lower your body temperature. Layer your clothing, protect your extremities, and find or create shelter. Use insulation like leaves or pine needles in your clothing and shelter.

- - WHAT TO DO WHEN YOU'RE ABOUT TO CROSS A FAST-MOVING RIVER - -

Look for the safest spot to cross - where the river is widest and slowest. Use a sturdy stick to test the depth and stability before each step. If it's too fast or too deep, find another spot to cross, or consider waiting until the water level drops.

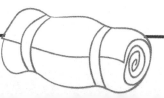

FALLEN INSECT FACTS

THE LETTERS OF THESE INTERESTING FACTS ABOUT INSECTS HAVE FALLEN OFF THE BOARD.
LUCKILY THEY LANDED DIRECTLY UNDER WHERE THEY BELONG.

13

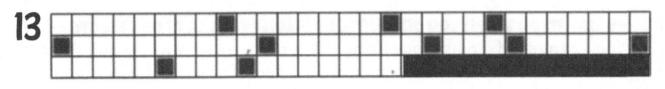

```
S T R R   O W       E I L E T   G                 M   E S
T H E I E N G T H   W L T F T S       O W O   M I M N S
H E R C U L E S N B E E I G H I N S H 8 5   I T   E     E
```

14

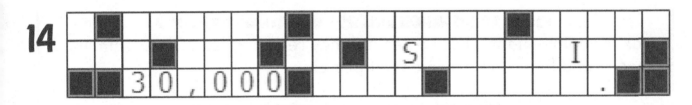

```
        S         L     T     A       T A   D
A   N I L A Y E   E G G M I O U N Q Y N G
C A     N G       A N E R S T D E I L U E E N
```

15

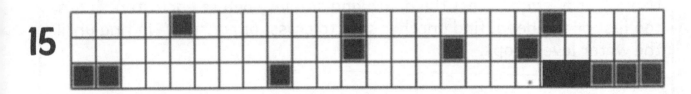

```
      B E   G R E   N U   F O C   I E     E
S N D E R O R C U S A   S P E C 1 7       A V S
U O M E F C I O A D D R F A R I N G S Y L I R E
```

37. Which bird species has the longest migration?
   A. Arctic Tern
   B. Red Knot
   C. Northern Pintail

38. What is the primary purpose of a tree's bark?
   A. Attracting insects
   B. Storing water
   C. Protecting the tree

39. What is the brightest star in the night sky?
   A. Polaris (North Star)
   B. Sirius (Dog Star)
   C. Vega

40. Which planet is known for its distinctive rings?
   A. Saturn
   B. Jupiter
   C. Uranus

41. What is the biggest species of shark in the world?
   A. Great White Shark
   B. Megalodon
   C. Whale Shark

42. Which river flows through the Grand Canyon?
   A. Colorado River
   B. Mississippi River
   C. Hudson River

43. What is the tallest tree species in the world?
   A. Giant Sequoia
   B. Coast Redwood
   C. Douglas Fir

44. What is the scientific term for animals that are active during the night?
   A. Diurnal
   B. Nocturnal
   C. Crepuscular

45. What causes a Rainbow?
   A. Reflection, refraction, and dispersion of light in water droplets
   B. Direct sunlight hitting moist air
   C. Reflection of sunlight off the moon

Puzzle #6 - Survival Skills

```
W Q H N G N I D L I U B G E V Y
U G L T O E A S G P H O A C L I
S M P I Y R C H H N Q O B E S Y
X E A D Y G T O S E I W Q Y Z C
S U L T F H N H R P L D X W G N
E G M E Z I E I L D K T N H U E
Q N R S C L R A K O A U E I A G
F I G E T T N S M C A G C R F R
I G S E T T I C T X A J E I B E
M A R K S A O O M A G R K P J M
R R N L F O W N N D I T T L Q E
E O D H K E K N I F E D M A R Z
T F V I Q M R K H C V B U N U Q
K U N M T I Z I Q V A I V T T L
W G Y H Z M S H F D X F J S G L
U K L S I G N A L I N G O Y H W
```

BUILDING   COOKING   CORDAGE
EMERGENCY   FINDING   FIRE
FIRST-AID   FORAGING   KNIFE
KNOT   NORTH   PLANTS
SELECTION   SHELTER   SIGNALING
TRACKING   WATER

Maze 6

WOULD U RATHER? - WILDLIFE ENCOUNTERS

1. Would you rather have a bird steal your hat or a monkey steal your food?

2. Would you rather share your campsite with a family of rabbits or a family of squirrels?

3. Would you rather encounter a friendly bear or an overly playful fox?

4. Would you rather hear wolves howling at night or see a snake slither by your campsite during the day?

5. Would you rather have a raccoon rummage through your stuff or a moose using your tent as a scratching post?

6. Would you rather be able to mimic any animal sound perfectly or have all animals understand your speech?

7. Would you rather get a visit from a curious deer or a shy turtle?

8. Would you rather wake up with a spider in your shoe or a mouse in your sleeping bag?

9. Would you rather be trailed by a harmless but persistent bear or accidentally step into a harmless but sticky anthill?

10. Would you rather have birds constantly poop on your tent or squirrels constantly gnawing on your backpack?

ROCKS AND MINERALS

ACROSS

4 The hardest known mineral, prized as a gemstone

5 A soft sulfate mineral composed of calcium sulfate dihydrate

7 A very hard, granular, crystalline, igneous rock

9 An ornamental mineral, mostly known for its green varieties

11 A blue gemstone variety of the mineral corundum

13 Sedimentary rock composed of sand-size grains of mineral, rock, or organic material

15 A precious stone, typically colorless, yellow, or pale blue, consisting of a fluorine-containing aluminum silicate

17 A hard, dark, glasslike volcanic rock formed by the rapid solidification of lava without crystallization

19 A violet or purple variety of quartz often used in jewelry

20 Metamorphic rock composed of recrystallized carbonate minerals

DOWN

1 A sedimentary rock, composed mainly of skeletal fragments of marine organisms

2 A shiny yellow mineral, FeS_2, having a faceted crystal form

3 A bright green precious stone consisting of a chromium-rich variety of beryl

6 One of the most common minerals in the Earth's crust

8 A small cavity in rock lined with crystals or other mineral matter

10 A mafic extrusive igneous rock formed from the rapid cooling of lava.

12 A precious stone consisting of corundum in color varieties varying from deep crimson or purple to pale rose

14 The remains or impression of a prehistoric organism preserved in petrified form

16 A gemstone known for its ability to diffract light

18 Fossilized tree resin, which is been appreciated for its color and natural beauty

CRYPTOGRAM 6

A	B	C	D	E	F	G	H	I	J	K	L	M

N	O	P	Q	R	S	T	U	V	W	X	Y	Z

M
_T_ R R B Y   M Q Y   O H Y

                      M   **M**
Z M Q A Y B O   T Y T P Y Q B

R S   O H Y   E Y Y Q

    M
S M T L Z C   .   O H Y L Q

    N   **N**   **N**
M U O Z Y Q B   D M U   B F M U

N F   O R   B L K   S Y Y O

                N
G L E Y   M U E   G Y L A H

              4 0   **N**
N F   O R   F R N U E B   .

DRAWING - ANIMAL CLOUDS

Look up at the clouds and find one that reminds you of an animal. Draw the cloud as you see it, then transform it into that animal in your drawing.

FALLEN INSECT FACTS

THE LETTERS OF THESE INTERESTING FACTS ABOUT INSECTS HAVE FALLEN OFF THE BOARD.
LUCKILY THEY LANDED DIRECTLY UNDER WHERE THEY BELONG.

16

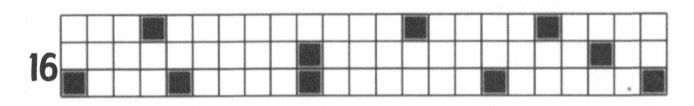

```
H R   A Z A S   I A A   N E   L   S
P A E A L E G G N   T L R I D T W K A E A T O
T L A Y T Y R E S T U N S A H A U T H W M S P
```

17

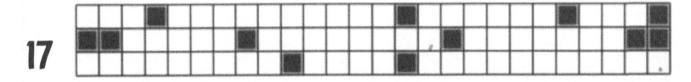

```
E   R O M   A   D H E R     E T L T   C A
T H E M I C A B S O W I E N   T E R E A E T I C D
C H S P B A Y L B R I L I N G B H C A U S E N E N
```

18

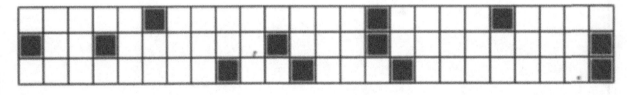

```
D F   S   A R     E E     H O E   J T
L 2 4 L H P M A Y F L I H N   L I V S T E U T
A I U E T O U N S O F T A S Y S I N R E C S S T
```

46. What is the largest landlocked country in the world?
    A. Mongolia
    B. Kazakhstan
    C. Bolivia

47. What is the smallest ocean in the world?
    A. Indian Ocean
    B. Arctic Ocean
    C. Southern Ocean

48. Which plant has the fastest growth rate?
    A. Sunflower
    B. Bamboo
    C. Ivy

49. What is the deepest canyon in the United States?
    A. Grand Canyon
    B. Hells Canyon
    C. Kings Canyon

50. Which mountain is closest to the moon due to the earth's equatorial bulge?
    A. Mount Everest
    B. Mount Kilimanjaro
    C. Mount Chimborazo

51. Which bird has the longest lifespan?
    A. Albatross
    B. Parrots (like the Cockatoo)
    C. Eagles

52. What is the largest freshwater lake in the world by volume?
    A. Lake Superior
    B. Lake Baikal
    C. Lake Michigan

53. Which species is the tallest bird in the world?
    A. Flamingo
    B. Ostrich
    C. Emu

54. Which planet has the strongest surface winds in the solar system?
    A. Venus
    B. Neptune
    C. Jupiter

Puzzle #7 - Starry Night Sky

```
E K N O I T A L L E T S N O C T
H T B Y B E C L I P S E K T I K
J V A V O N R E P U S A A B N I
A S T R O N O M Y E D V R R V F
L K M J D J N W B T D O A H E A
T T P E S O M S O C P L H X L
U Z T L P L V V N I O M W N Y U
A G S C A O B J T S I E U M J B
N Z U P E N C D M E X T X O L E
O Z Z N A L E S Y K M E I G U N
R N G J I C E T E S B O W A N C
T W O Q S V E S S L J R C L A L
S D L O F H E F T P E H O A R P
A G Q K M I N R R I G T D X P E
V G I Y B N U S S R A T S Y N E
N L D K K U Q I I E M L D R I Z
```

ASTRONAUT	ASTRONOMY	CELESTIAL
COMET	CONSTELLATION	COSMOS
ECLIPSE	GALAXY	LUNAR
METEOR	MOON	NEBULA
ORBIT	PLANETS	SOLAR
SPACE	STARS	SUPERNOVA
TELESCOPE	UNIVERSE	

Maze 7

WOULD U RATHER? - ADVENTURE

1. Would you rather explore a hidden cave or climb a towering tree?

2. Would you rather discover a secret waterfall or a hidden meadow filled with wildflowers?

3. Would you rather go on a treasure hunt or a nature scavenger hunt?

4. Would you rather spend the day hiking up a mountain or paddling down a river?

5. Would you rather navigate through a dense forest or scale a rocky hill?

6. Would you rather find a mysterious map or an old, fascinating artifact?

7. Would you rather be able to see all the hidden paths in the forest or be able to see at night as clearly as in the day?

8. Would you rather explore a beautiful coral reef or a majestic old-growth forest?

9. Would you rather find a secret treehouse or a hidden cave behind a waterfall?

10. Would you rather trek through the wilderness or ride through on a mountain bike?

WHAT'S BUGGING YOU?

ACROSS

1 Often nocturnal insect attracted to light, related to the butterfly.

3 Flying insect known for its sting, often builds nests from paper-like material.

6 Hard to kill insect often found in human habitats, known as a pest.

11 Jumping insect that makes a chirping sound, often found in fields.

12 Insect known for its brightly colored wings and transformation from a caterpillar.

15 Eight-legged arachnid that spins webs to catch its prey.

16 Social insect known for feeding on wood and damaging buildings.

18 Small flightless insect known for jumping and feeding on the blood of mammals.

19 Predatory insect with large eyes and long body, often seen near water.

21 Common household insect known for its ability to spread diseases.

22 Insect known for its ability to produce light in its abdomen.

23 Insect that resembles twigs as a form of camouflage.

DOWN

1 Flying insect known for its biting and ability to transmit diseases.

2 Small arachnid that feeds on the blood of mammals, often found in tall grass.

4 Small sap-sucking insect that's often considered a pest in gardens.

5 Small nocturnal insect that feeds on human blood, often found in beds.

7 Small, social insect that often lives in complex colonies.

8 A type of grasshopper that can form large swarms and devastate crops.

9 The larval stage of butterflies and moths, often seen munching on leaves.

10 Hard-shelled insect that's among the most diverse group of animals on Earth.

13 Insect known for its role in pollination and producing honey.

14 Small round and often red insect with black spots, beneficial as they eat pests.

17 Known for its prayer-like stance, a predatory insect that eats other insects.

20 Small flying insect, often forms large swarms.

A	B	C	D	E	F	G	H	I	J	K	L	M

N	O	P	Q	R	S	T	U	V	W	X	Y	Z

```
_   _   E   E   _
L   U   S   S   G

_   _   _   _   _   _   _   _   _   E   _       _   _   _   _
M   I   R   R   Y   A   O   M   B   L   S       C   O   L   N

E   _   _   _       _   _   E   _   !
S   B   M   N       I   L   N   S   U

_   _   _   _   _   _   _       _   _
L   N   U   I   Y   P   N       B   A

_   _   D   E   _   _   _   _   _   D
Y   A   Z   S   U   P   U   I   Y   A   Z

_   E   _   _   _   _   _   _
A   S   L   C   I   U   F       I   K

_   _   _   _   _   ,   _   _   E   E   _       _   _   _
K   Y   A   P   O       L   U   S   S   G       M   B   A

_   E   _   D   _   _   _   E   _   _   _   _
G   S   A   Z       M   N   S   R   O   M   B   X

_   _   _   _   _   _   _       _   _   _   _   _
G   O   P   A   B   X   G       L   I   C   B   U   A

E   _   _   _       _   _   E   _   _   _   _
S   B   M   N       I   L   N   S   U       I   K

D   _   _   _   E   _   .
Z   B   A   P   S   U   G
```

Scavenger Hunt-rocks
Find 8 different shaped or colored rocks
Draw or trace them

Puzzle #8 - Birds of Prey

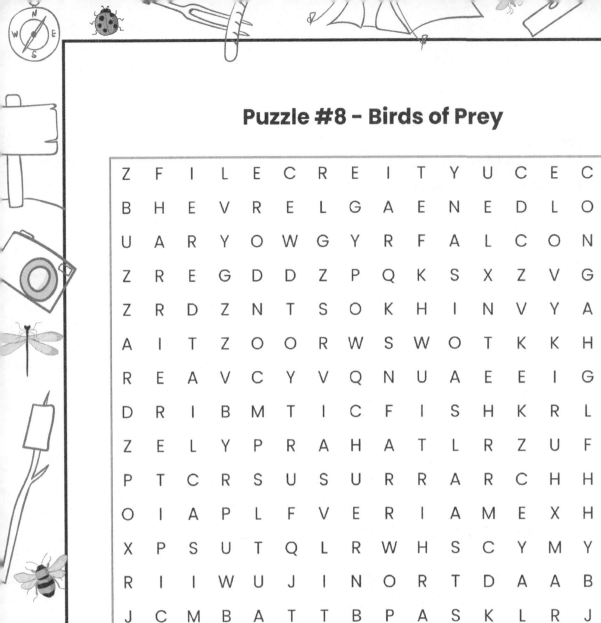

```
Z  F  I  L  E  C  R  E  I  T  Y  U  C  E  C  Y
B  H  E  V  R  E  L  G  A  E  N  E  D  L  O  G
U  A  R  Y  O  W  G  Y  R  F  A  L  C  O  N  H
Z  R  E  G  D  D  Z  P  Q  K  S  X  Z  V  G  U
Z  R  D  Z  N  T  S  O  K  H  I  N  V  Y  A  S
A  I  T  Z  O  O  R  W  S  W  O  T  K  K  H  Y
R  E  A  V  C  Y  V  Q  N  U  A  E  E  I  G  P
D  R  I  B  M  T  I  C  F  I  S  H  K  R  L  U
Z  E  L  Y  P  R  A  H  A  T  L  R  Z  U  F  J
P  T  C  R  S  U  S  U  R  R  A  R  C  H  H  K
O  I  A  P  L  F  V  E  R  I  A  M  E  X  H  W
X  P  S  U  T  Q  L  R  W  H  S  C  Y  M  Y  A
R  I  I  W  U  J  I  N  O  R  T  D  A  A  B  H
J  C  M  B  A  T  T  B  P  A  S  K  L  R  J  S
Y  C  A  M  L  Q  B  O  G  U  F  B  D  M  A  O
I  A  Q  W  C  Y  U  G  R  P  N  O  S  E  I  G
```

ACCIPITER	BUZZARD	CARACARA
CONDOR	GOLDEN EAGLE	GOSHAWK
GYRFALCON	HARPY	HARRIER
HAWK	HOBBY	KESTREL
KITE	MERLIN	OSPREY
REDTAIL	SHIKRA	TIERCEL

Maze 8

WOULD U RATHER? - CAMPING COMFORT

1. Would you rather camp with no change of clothes for a week or no shower for a week?

2. Would you rather sleep in a sleeping bag that's too small or in a tent that's too big?

3. Would you rather have only cold food to eat or only cold drinks to drink?

4. Would you rather camp in a luxurious RV or in a primitive lean-to?

5. Would you rather have no toilet paper for a week or no toothpaste for a week?

6. Would you rather cook every meal over a campfire or eat only pre-packaged camping food?

7. Would you rather have your flashlight run out of batteries in the middle of the night or your compass break while you're hiking?

8. Would you rather always have smelly feet or always have a sunburn?

9. Would you rather sleep on a rocky ground or under a leaky tent?

10. Would you rather have a noisy neighbor at the next campsite or have mosquitoes buzzing around your tent all night?

STARS AND CONSTELLATIONS

ACROSS

2 Our home galaxy
5 The brightest star in the night sky
8 The largest planet in the solar system
11 An open star cluster, also known as 'The Seven Sisters'
14 A constellation named after a princess in Greek mythology, known for its galaxy
15 A small body of matter from outer space that enters the earth's atmosphere, appearing as a streak of light
17 A system of millions or billions of stars, together with gas and dust
18 Also known as the North Star
19 Second planet from the sun, also known as the Evening Star
20 An event in which a celestial body is obscured by another

DOWN

1 A region of space having a gravitational field so intense that no matter or radiation can escape
3 A natural light display in the Earth's sky, predominantly seen in the polar regions
4 A celestial object consisting of a nucleus of ice and dust and, when near the sun, a 'tail' of gas and dust particles
6 A star that suddenly increases greatly in brightness because of a catastrophic explosion
7 Also known as the Great Bear
9 A prolific meteor shower associated with the comet Swift-Tuttle
10 An instrument used for observing distant objects.
12 The winged horse of Greek mythology that forms a constellation
13 A cloud of gas and dust in outer space
16 Known as 'The Hunter', easily recognizable by its 'belt' of three stars in a row

CRYPTOGRAM 8

A	B	C	D	E	F	G	H	I	J	K	L	M

N	O	P	Q	R	S	T	U	V	W	X	Y	Z

_ _ _ _ _ _ **N** _ _ **S** _
O N C R U L Q C H O

_ _ _ _ _ _ _ _ _ _ _ _ _ **N** _
W C Z U W B C B N F A F L Q

_ _ _ _ _ _ **N** _ _ _
O W J F R F L O N C

_ _ _ _ _ _ **S** _ _ _
K U W R B F H O N C

_ _ _ _ _ _ _ _ _ **S** _ _
M J Z F I F Z Z W C H O

_ _ _ _ _ , _ _ _ _ _
O W J F R K N F Z N

S _ _ **N** **S** _ _ _ _ 2 , 6 5 0
H M J L H U D C W

_ _ _ _ **S** _ _ _ _ _
X F R C H I W U X

_ _ _ _ _ _ _ _
X C E F Z U O U

_ _ **N** _ _ _ .
Z J L J B J

DRAWING - CAMPSITE MAP

Draw a bird's-eye view of your campsite, including your tent, fire pit, nearby trees, and any other notable features. Then, imagine and draw what might be hidden beneath the surface - an underground network of animal burrows, or buried treasure.

Puzzle #9 – Campfire Songs

```
L V G N I P M A C W T Y E N V B
F Y R E T H G U A L D W X X E K
C E R L A M W Y F O S R A S K R
I X S I D A N R L O F K A I R E
Y M L M C U R E Y D L C Q N P H
V I E U K S M Y X T B K D G O T
F N R S O D H C U A K Y X I J E
Q C I I L R A W J A O I S N J G
C I F C Y T R P R J U Z T G K O
F T P J C F M I Q R A T I U G T
I S M B X D O F R I E N D S O C
F U A N F G N V V D E F H W J G
V O C S Z Q Y C S I N G I N G I
Z C C H O R U S A O L C Z R H V
G A D P Q O Y X F N I G H T E U
B B J O T M M E M O R I E S L N
```

ACOUSTIC	CAMPFIRE	CAMPING
CHORUS	FIRE	FOLK
FRIENDS	GUITAR	HARMONY
JOY	LAUGHTER	LYRICS
MELODY	MEMORIES	MUSIC
NIGHT	SINGING	TOGETHER

Maze 9

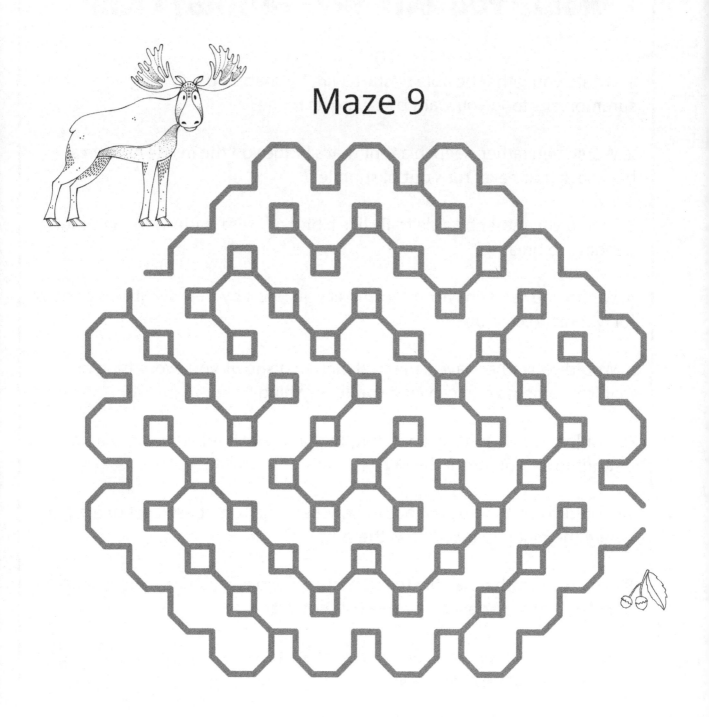

WOULD YOU RATHER? - FANTASY CAMP

1. Would you rather be able to start a fire by snapping your fingers or summon any food you want by saying its name?

2. Would you rather sleep in a tent that's bigger on the inside or have a backpack that never runs out of supplies?

3. Would you rather be able to fly like a bird or swim underwater without needing to breathe?

4. Would you rather have your campsite guarded by friendly ghosts or helpful woodland creatures?

5. Would you rather have a magical map that shows you everything or a magical compass that can lead you to anything?

6. Would you rather have a pet dragon that could light your campfire or a pet griffin to scout from the sky?

7. Would you rather experience a day where the sun doesn't set or a night where the moon is as bright as the sun?

8. Would you rather be able to teleport to any place you've seen in a picture or be able to time travel to any era of the past?

9. Would you rather have your own enchanted forest or a magical river that can change into any beverage?

10. Would you rather have a mystical creature as a companion or a magical item that can do incredible things?

CRYPTOGRAM 9

A	B	C	D	E	F	G	H	I	J	K	L	M

N	O	P	Q	R	S	T	U	V	W	X	Y	Z
	O											

K L F W Y T L T F   E O T

A Y R L B G   Y W G   A O H G

M K O E G   Y P L E G '   O T Z

Y R G G A   O R G   D V Y G T
        O

Y W G   R G E L M L G T Y A .

Y W L A   L A   I G E O S A G
               U

Y R G G A   O E Y   O A

T O Y S R O K
   U

K L F W Y T L T F   R D Z A .
               O

CRYPTOGRAM 10

A	B	C	D	E	F	G	H	I	J	K	L	M

N	O	P	Q	R	S	T	U	V	W	X	Y	Z

_ E _   _ E _ _ _
X I A   B A V E H

_ _ _ _ _ _ _ '   _ _
G F L X Y U W   U

_ _ _ _ I _ _ _ _ _ _
O U Y V M B J Y J E H

_ _ _ _ ' _ _ _   _ _ _ _ E
W F U V X   O U V   O F J H A

I _ _   _ _ _ _   I _   _ E _ _
M X H   X Y U W   M V   F A H H

_ _ _ _   _   H E _ _ _ _
X I U V   U   H A O J V T

_ _ _ E _   _ _ I _ _ E _ _ E _
N I A V   X Y M C C A Y A T

_ _ _   _   _ _ _ .
S L U   U   S E C

WHAT TO DO WHEN...

Take turns with someone else at camp to see if you know the
best way to handle these wilderness survival situations.

- - WHAT TO DO WHEN YOU'RE CAUGHT IN A LIGHTNING STORM - -

Seek shelter immediately, but avoid standing near tall trees or other high points that may attract lightning. If there's no available shelter, make yourself as small a target as possible by crouching low to the ground on the balls of your feet.

- - WHAT TO DO WHEN YOU'RE OUT OF MATCHES OR A LIGHTER - -

Try alternative fire starting methods. You could use a flint and steel, a friction-based method like a bow drill, or even the battery-and-steel-wool method.

- - WHAT TO DO WHEN YOU SUSPECT HYPOTHERMIA - -

Get out of the cold, remove any wet clothing, and get dry and warm as quickly as possible. Consume warm, high-energy foods and drinks if available.

- - WHAT TO DO WHEN A BLIZZARD STRIKES - -

Try to find or build a shelter that will protect you from the wind and snow. Stay put until the blizzard has passed to avoid getting lost or injured.

- - WHAT TO DO WHEN YOU COME ACROSS A SNAKE - -

Give the snake a wide berth - most snake bites occur when someone tries to handle or harm the snake. If bitten, try to remember the snake's appearance, keep calm, limit movement, and seek medical attention immediately.

Puzzle #10 - Weather or Not

```
H M T U M Q D T U F S Q J F N N
V E R H M U Y Z S T H Y P K W K
D N U O E D D G H C O A U S O V
L D U U T T L U L O D M Y H B D
L B V S S S N O E F I Q B O N J
R T V U R D U W O L M P Y U I G
U B G W E D C G M C Z H V V A Z
O R X R S D C S H Y A Z D D R G
P E S D N R W X L I Y X I R J N
N E F I S A K F L E V I A R J A
W Z W F N Z T F L D E I C N D E
O E S X O Z Z E R N T W N F T
D Q U Q W I H U R R I C A N E I
E O J C T L X R O D A N R O T K
G F D Z Y B T S I M K D L C G Z
Y S U R S C L I G H T N I N G Z
```

BLIZZARD	BREEZE	CLOUDS
DOWNPOUR	DRIZZLE	FOG
GUST	HAIL	HURRICANE
LIGHTNING	MIST	RAIN
RAINBOW	SLEET	SNOW
STORM	SUN	THUNDER
TORNADO	WIND	

Maze 10

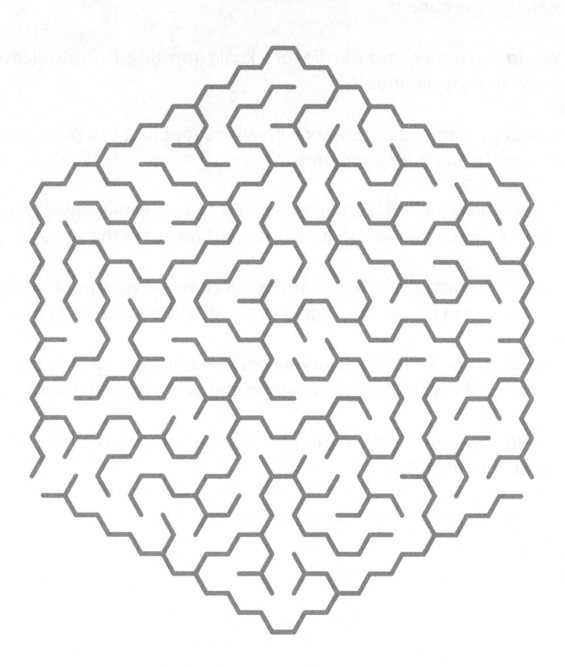

WOULD U RATHER? - MIXUP 1

Would you rather be a spider with fear of small spaces or a bat that is scared of the dark?

Would you rather have the diet of a koala (mostly eucalyptus leaves) or a panda (mostly bamboo)?

Would you rather eat a burger with all the toppings but no bun or a hot dog with a bun but no toppings?

Would you rather drink a cup of melt ed campfire marshmallow goo or a cup of melted ice cream that has been sitting out in the sun all day?

Would you rather wake up to all of your camping gear mysteriously rear-ranged or find cryptic messages written in the dirt around your campsite?

Would you rather hear a knock on your tent in the middle of the night or find a set of keys that don't belong to you or anyone in your group?

Would you rather camp in a dense forest full of bugs or on a windy, barren mountain?

Would you rather have a campfire that can't be put out or not be allowed to light a fire at all?

CRYPTOGRAM 11

A	B	C	D	E	F	G	H	I	J	K	L	M

N	O	P	Q	R	S	T	U	V	W	X	Y	Z

```
_   _ _ _ _ _   _ _   _ _ _ S
V   O Z H F E   H M   H Y K P

_ S   _ _ _ _ _ _   _
A P   R V K K U L   V

_ _ _ _ _ _ _ T _ .
E V Z K A V X U T D

T _ _ S _   _ _ S _   _ _ _ _ S
D J U P U   Y A P U   Q A Z L P

_ _ _   _ _ _ _   _ _ _
V Z U   S T H Y T   M H Z

T _ _ _ _
D J U A Z

_ _ _ _ _ T _ _ _ _ _
U W R U E D A H T V K

_ _ _ _ T _   _ _ S _ _ _   _ _ _
T A O J D   B A P A H T   V T L

S _ _ _ _ _   T _ _ _ T .
P A K U T D   M K A O J D
```

CRYPTOGRAM 12

A	B	C	D	E	F	G	H	I	J	K	L	M

N	O	P	Q	R	S	T	U	V	W	X	Y	Z

_ _ _ _ **N** _ _   _ _ **N** _
X W F P L V S   W V C

_ _ _ **N** _ _ _ **N** _   _ _ _ _   _ **N**
H P N V C L V S   B L F N   L V

N _ _ _ _ _   _ _ _ _   _ _ **N**
V W B Z I N   Q W T N   U N N V

_ _ _ _ _ **N** _ _ _ _ _ _ _ _
H X L N V B L J L X W D D O

_ _ **O** _ _ _   _ **N**   _ **O**   _ _ _ _ _
P I R T N V   B R   I N C Z X N

_ _ _ _ _ _ _   _ _ _ _ _ _
H B I N H H   D N T N D H

_ **N** _   _ **O** **O** _ _   _ **O** **O** _ .
W V C   U R R H B   F R R C

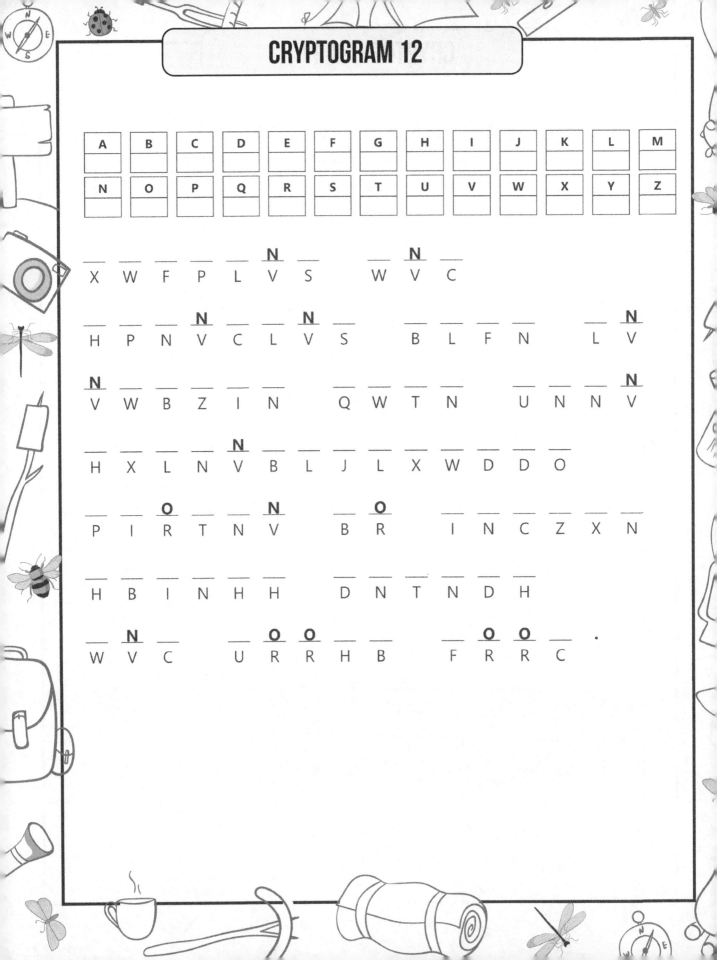

DRAWING - STARRY SKY CREATURE

If you're camping under a clear night sky, find a constellation and draw the stars as you see them. Then, connect the dots to create your own creature or character.

Puzzle #11 - Knots and Ropes

```
W Q T E L P I R T I O R T R S A
D P R U S I K Q P D I E E O X H
N Y X R U O E E D K B B E T Y R
Y E L X O S G K C S T M H C L H
F N W A T E R W E J G I S I F S
I I G Q H Y V O R N V T Z R R R
S P D H C Q E O E D J G R T E E
H L A W L W L K L N E K S S T K
E A C D S L T F N C I L R N T C
R N N Y I Q C A B O I L N O U U
M E S N Z C U L U P M L W C B R
A Y G A J Y F A B T P Q Z O V T
N W G M G U U P R Z L S F K B T
P A D J O F G P H E W I H W V O
R E Q D A E H S K R A L N N G C
Z E P P E L I N V M R R C E I L
```

ALPINE	BOWLINE	BUTTERFLY
CLOVE	CONSTRICTOR	FISHERMAN
LARKS HEAD	MONKEY	PRUSIK
ROLLING	SHEET	SLIP
SQUARE	TAUTLINE	TIMBER
TRIPLE	TRUCKERS	WATER
ZEPPELIN		

Maze 11

WOULD U RATHER? - MIXUP 2

Would you rather swim with friendly fish or dance with playful butterflies?

Would you rather have a noisy woodpecker nearby your tent or a stinky skunk as your neighbor?

Would you rather discover a new species of animal or a new type of plant?

Would you rather cross a desert on a camel or a snowy landscape on a sled?

Would you rather accidentally pack a winter sleeping bag in the summer or a summer sleeping bag in the winter?

Would you rather forget to bring your favorite book or your favorite snack?

Would you rather be able to talk to trees or control the weather?

Would you rather find a magic lamp with a genie or a magic wand with unlimited spells?

Would you rather wake up to see a majestic eagle perched nearby or find a rare flower blooming next to your tent?

Would you rather be able to control the weather at your campsite or make food grow on trees?

CRYPTOGRAM 13

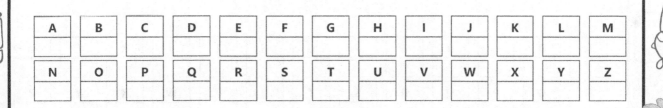

A	B	C	D	E	F	G	H	I	J	K	L	M

N	O	P	Q	R	S	T	U	V	W	X	Y	Z

T _ _   _ _ I _ _ _ I _
W T Z   E T O X D O Y R

_ _ _ _ _   _ _
B M N Y I   M H

_ _ I _ _ _ T _   _ I _
E X O E V Z W B   O B

_ _ T _ _ _ _ _   T _ _
G E W N G F F K   W T Z

_ _ _ _ _   _ I _ _ I _   _ T _
P G F Z B   B O Y R O Y R   W M

_ T T _ _ _ T   _ _ _ _ _ _ _ .
G W W X G E W   H Z P G F Z B

T _ _   _ _ T T _ _ _   _ _ _
W T Z   D G W W Z X Y   G Y I

_ _ _ _ _   _ _   T _ _ I _
B D Z Z I   M H   W T Z O X

_ I _ _ _ _   _ _ _   _ _ _ _ .
E T O X D B   E G Y   U G X K

CRYPTOGRAM 14

A	B	C	D	E	F	G	H	I	J	K	L	M

N	O	P	Q	R	S	T	U	V	W	X	Y	Z

_ _ E _ _ _ _ S _ _ _ _ _ _ E _ E ,
O Y W   N P T Y V Q   O J W W

_ _ _ _ _ _ E _ _ _ _
Q   V R G K V W   Q R E

_ _ _ _ _ _ _ _ _ _
G C P R G C   S A Q R O

_ _ _ _ _ _ _ _ _ E
Z P V R E   G R   O Y W

_ _ _ _ _ E _ _ E S E _ _ ,
F P N Q H W   E W T W J O

_ _ _ _ E _ _ _ _ _
C Q R   A G H W   Z P J

_ _ _ _ E _ _ S _ _
Y V R E J W E T   P Z

_ E _ _ _ S _ _ _ _ _ _ _
U W Q J T   Q R E   C Q R   O P

_ _ _ _ _ _ _ _ 4 0
L J P D   V S   O P

_ E _ E _ _ _ _ _ .
Z W W O   O Q A A

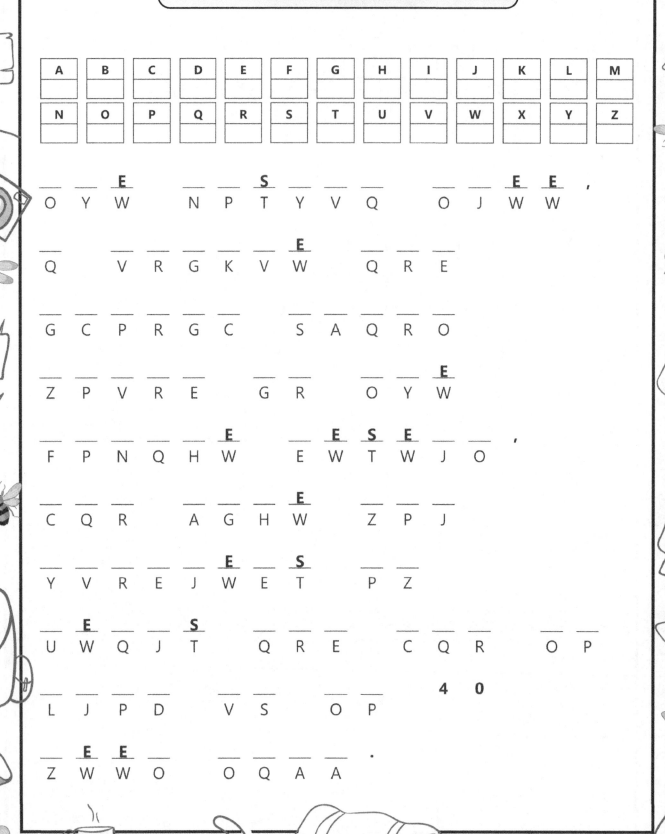

Scavenger Hunt- Insects

Find 8 different insects
Draw them in the spaces below

Puzzle #12 – Wildflowers

```
G M I L K W E E D M N H O W X F
R D E N I B M U L O C S R X S F
X R U D B E C K I A S U C N B E
S U N F L O W E R J Q R H M D R
W Y S P R I M R O S E B I M T J
U D J R E T S A O B K T D E N F
C O N E F L O W E R E N I P U L
R R M U I L L I R T W I A R W A
O F U A A V A S Y O A A L O O X
S Z M T H T F C P S I P R G Z E
J P H L O X B S P E K R G U U P
A Z N N V M J R O D A J S N I D
N H O K M Y W C P Y U V K D X G
I B E R G A M O T L K X X D L T
A I L E B O L I D S N R X Q M S
P I G R V Q H V F I R E W E E D
```

ASTER	BERGAMOT	COLUMBINE
CONEFLOWER	FIREWEED	LOBELIA
LUPINE	MILKWEED	ORCHID
PAINTBRUSH	PHLOX	POPPY
PRIMROSE	RUDBECKIA	SUNFLOWER
TRILLIUM	YARROW	

Maze 12

FALLEN INSECT FACTS

THE LETTERS OF THESE INTERESTING FACTS ABOUT INSECTS HAVE FALLEN OFF THE BOARD.
LUCKILY THEY LANDED DIRECTLY UNDER WHERE THEY BELONG.

19

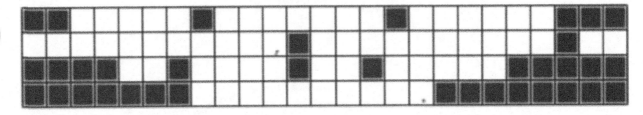

```
      E E     T T
   I E   S I N D   T O E E E A D I
S N A T K P I S S E P R S T V M D E N Y
T H A T B C O D R A D A C O R S E N P L O G   T O
```

20

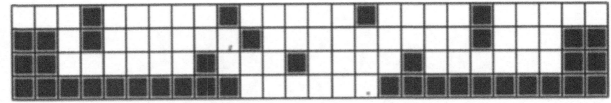

```
            T   A R
   E   O R E T   A T U G V   M   T A   V A F
   A   M O A N T   A T A R E I V I L G   O F C
T H S T G I U D H F S S L F S O M O N H R L A L K S
```

CRYPTOGRAM 15

N	O	P	Q	R	S	T	U	V	W	X	Y	Z

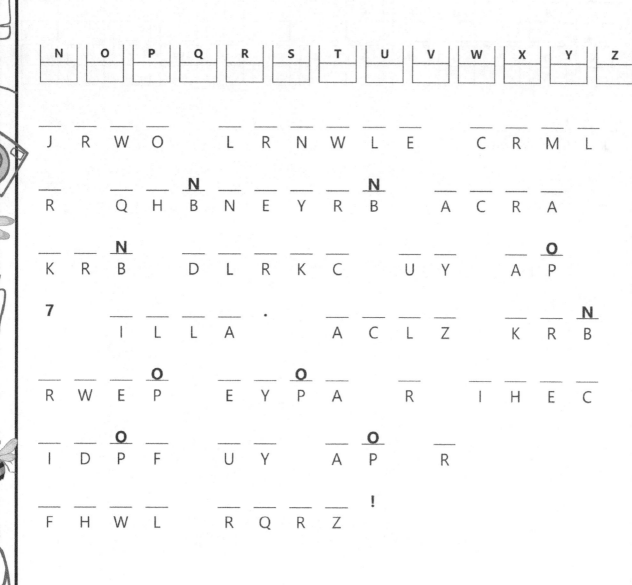

J R W O   L R N W L E   C R M L

_ _ _ **N** _ _ _ _ **N** _ _ _ _
R Q H B N E Y R B   A C R A

_ **N** _ _ _ _ _ _ _ _ **O** _
K R B D L R K C   U Y   A P

7 _ _ _ _ . _ _ _ _ _ **N**
  I L L A   A C L Z   K R B

_ _ **O** _ _ _ **O** _ _ _ _ _ _
R W E P   E Y P A   R   I H E C

_ _ **O** _ _ _ _ **O** _ _
I D P F   U Y   A P   R

_ _ _ _ _ _ _ _ !
F H W L   R Q R Z

CRYPTOGRAM 16

A	B	C	D	E	F	G	H	I	J	K	L	M

N	O	P	Q	R	S	T	U	V	W	X	Y	Z

K A Y B Q F M   K U L W Y E

Q L V F   E K F B A L U A I F J

U F L V F E   Y Q L Y   N D M C

L   " K A Y B Q F M "

E Q L K F ,   N A U U F J

S A Y Q   L   E Y A B R T

U A H P A J   Y Q L Y

Y M L K E

P W E P E K F B Y A W X

G P X E .

WHAT TO DO WHEN...

Take turns with someone else at camp to see if you know the best way to handle these wilderness survival situations.

- - WHAT TO DO WHEN YOU NEED TO MOVE ACROSS DIFFICULT TERRAIN - -

Use a walking stick for extra stability. Walk at a steady, manageable pace to conserve energy. Plan your route to avoid unnecessary risks and exertion.

- - WHAT TO DO WHEN YOU NEED TO SIGNAL FOR HELP BUT YOU'VE LOST YOUR WHISTLE OR FLARE - -

Use what you have available. Create a smoky fire by adding green leaves or plastic to your fire, use a mirror or shiny object to reflect sunlight, or create a large, visible signal on the ground using rocks or branches.

- - WHAT TO DO WHEN YOU'RE CAUGHT IN A FOREST FIRE - -

Stay calm, and move away from the fire as quickly and safely as possible. If there's a body of water nearby, move toward it. Don't try to outrun a fire uphill, as heat rises and can spread quickly.

- - WHAT TO DO WHEN YOU'RE STUCK IN QUICKSAND OR MUD - -

Try to distribute your weight evenly across the surface. Do not struggle violently; instead, move slowly and deliberately, leaning back and trying to float on the surface. Use any tools or long objects available to help pull yourself out.

- - WHAT TO DO WHEN YOU ENCOUNTER A BEAR - -

Avoid direct eye contact, which the bear might interpret as a threat. Speak in a calm, assertive voice and slowly back away without turning your back on the bear. Do not run, as this may trigger a chase response.

CRYPTOGRAM 17

A	B	C	D	E	F	G	H	I	J	K	L	M

N	O	P	Q	R	S	T	U	V	W	X	Y	Z

T _ _   _ _ _ _ _ _ .
T J W   K E G V L S

_ _ _ _ _ _ **T**   _ _ _ _ ,
V F G A W S T   M F X W

_ _ _   _ _ _ _   _ _ _ _ '
S E H   L E E H A   M F X W

_ _   _ _   _ _ _ _ _ _ _
Q S   S E   I F S S Q X W

T _ _ **T**   _ **T**   _ _ _   _ **T** _
T J F T   Q T   J F S   Q T S

_ _ _   _ _ _ **T** _ _ _
E K H   K W F T J W G

_ _ _ **T** _ _ '   _ _ _ _ _ _ **T** _
S N S T W I   M E I U V W T W

_ _ **T** _   _ _ _ _ _ _   _ _ _
K Q T J   M V E C L S   F H L

_ _ _ _ _ _
C H Q O C W

_ _ _ _ _ _ **T** _ _ _ _ .
W M E S N S T W I S

DRAWING - NATURE'S PORTRAIT

Find a tree, a plant, or a flower that catches your eye. Draw it as realistically as you can, capturing all the details. Then, give it a face and personality - imagine it as a character and bring it to life.

CRYPTOGRAM 18

A	B	C	D	E	F	G	H	I	J	K	L	M

N	O	P	Q	R	S	T	U	V	W	X	Y	Z

L   Y F L T   J L W

I F Q F J Q   M J F W Q M
                     S   S

C T U N   G B   Q U   2 0

N H V F M   L E L K ,
            S

N L Z H W O   H Q

H N B U T Q L W Q   Q U

M Q U T F   C U U I
S

B T U B F T V K   E S F W

J L N B H W O   H W   Y F L T

J U G W Q T K .

CRYPTOGRAM 19

A	B	C	D	E	F	G	H	I	J	K	L	M
N	O	P	Q	R	S	T	U	V	W	X	Y	Z

_ _ **E** _ _ **E** _ _
N V M   W O M U N

_ _ _ _ **E** _ _   _ **E** **E** _   _ _
G U O O F M O   O M M B   F E

_ _ _ _ _ _ _ _   _ _   _ _ **E**
U T J N O U X F U   F J   N V M

_ _ _ _ **E** _ _   _ _ _ _ _
X U O W M J N   X F C F E W

_ _ _ _ _ _ **E** _   _ _
J N O T S N T O M   P E

E _ _ _ _   _ _ _   _ _
M U O N V   U E D   F J

_ _ _ _ _ _ **E** _   _ _ _ _
C F J F G X M   B O P A

_ _ _ _ **E** .   _ _   _ _
J Y U S M   F N   F J

_ _ _ **E** _ _   _ _   _ _ _ _ _
A U D M   T Y   P B   S P O U X

_ _ _ _ _ _ .
Y P X H Y J

CRYPTOGRAM 20

A	B	C	D	E	F	G	H	I	J	K	L	M

N	O	P	Q	R	S	T	U	V	W	X	Y	Z

J Q U L J V Q L B

D U G X O H L   V Q C M R

R M U G O C M   <u>A</u> K

D U G H L B B   H <u>A</u> K V V L X

P Q G V O N Q S L B H L S H L   .   -

R M L E   O B L   R M Q B

V Q C M R   R G

H G N N O S Q H <u>A</u> K R L   <u>A</u> K S X

<u>A</u> K R R U <u>A</u> K H R   N <u>A</u> K R L B .

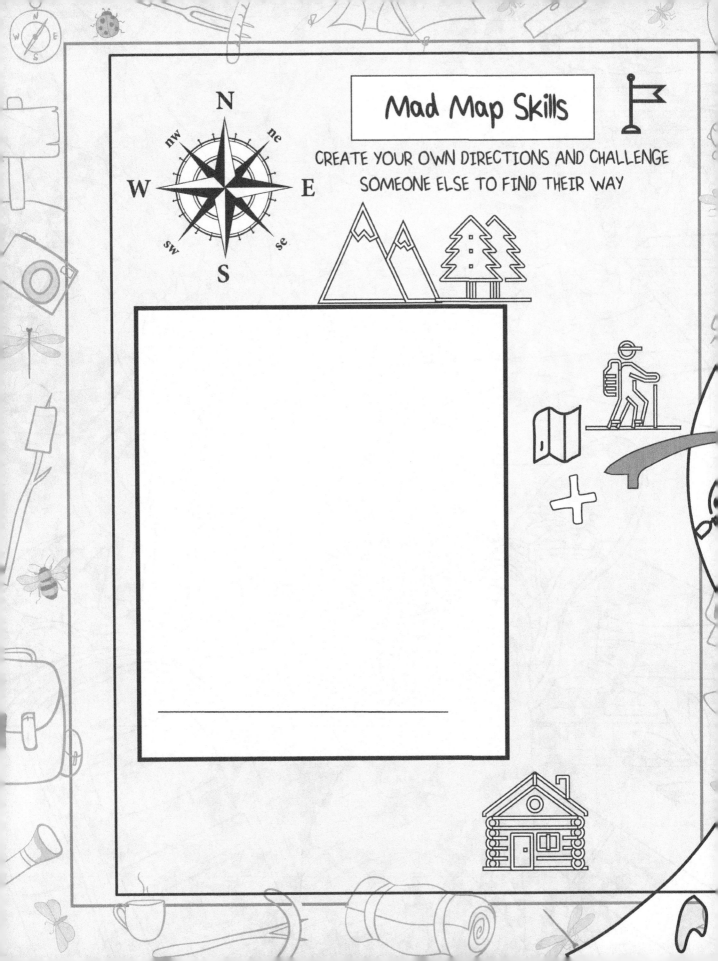

Mad Map Skills

CREATE YOUR OWN DIRECTIONS AND CHALLENGE
SOMEONE ELSE TO FIND THEIR WAY

Mad Map Skills

CREATE YOUR OWN DIRECTIONS AND CHALLENGE
SOMEONE ELSE TO FIND THEIR WAY

DOTS

HANGMAN

A	B	C	D
E	F	G	H
I	J	K	L	M
N	O	P	Q
R	S	T	U
V	W	X	Y	Z

A	B	C	D
E	F	G	H
I	J	K	L	M
N	O	P	Q
R	S	T	U
V	W	X	Y	Z

ROCK, PAPER, SCISSORS
BEST OF 11 ROUNDS WINS

ROUND	PLAYER 1	PLAYER 2
1		
2		
3		
4		
5		
6		
7		
8		
9		
10		
11		

WINNER - _____

TIC TAC TOE

WINNER (BEST OF
11 ROUNDS)

_____

DOTS

HANGMAN

ROCK, PAPER, SCISSORS
BEST OF 11 ROUNDS WINS

ROUND	PLAYER 1	PLAYER 2
1		
2		
3		
4		
5		
6		
7		
8		
9		
10		
11		

WINNER - _____

TIC TAC TOE

WINNER (BEST OF
11 ROUNDS)

_____

DOTS

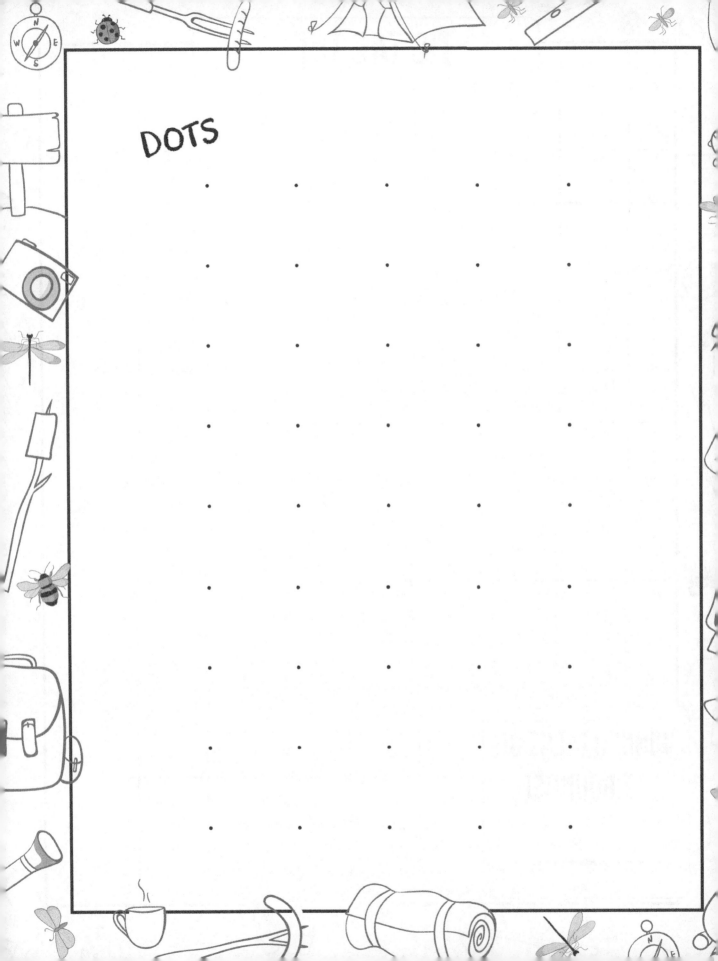

HANGMAN

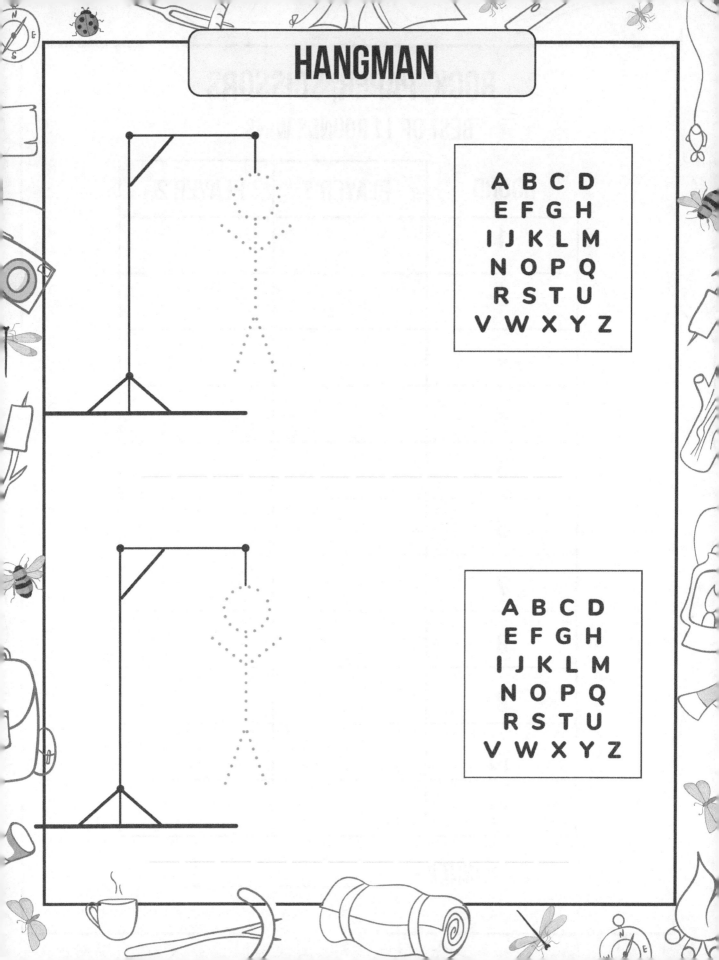

A B C D
E F G H
I J K L M
N O P Q
R S T U
V W X Y Z

A B C D
E F G H
I J K L M
N O P Q
R S T U
V W X Y Z

ROCK, PAPER, SCISSORS
BEST OF 11 ROUNDS WINS

ROUND	PLAYER 1	PLAYER 2
1		
2		
3		
4		
5		
6		
7		
8		
9		
10		
11		

WINNER - _____

TIC TAC TOE

WINNER (BEST OF 11 ROUNDS)

_____

ANSWERS

Puzzle #1 - Haunted Campfire Stories - Solution

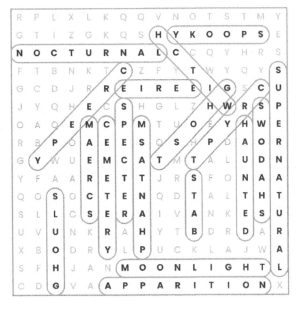

Puzzle #2 - Outdoor Activities - Solution

Puzzle #3 - Campfire Foods - Solution

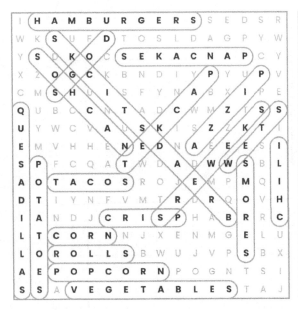

Puzzle #4 - National Parks - Solution

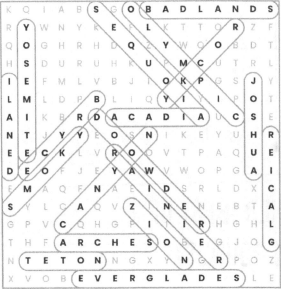

ANSWERS

Puzzle #5 - Hiking Trails - Solution

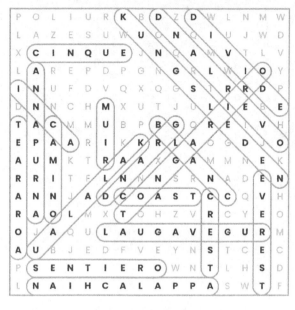

Puzzle #6 - Survival Skills - Solution

Puzzle #7 - Starry Night Sky - Solution

Puzzle #8 - Birds of Prey - Solution

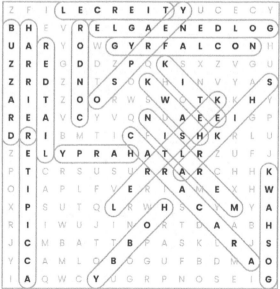

Puzzle #9 - Campfire Songs - Solution

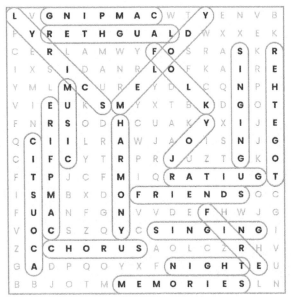

Puzzle #10 - Weather or Not - Solution

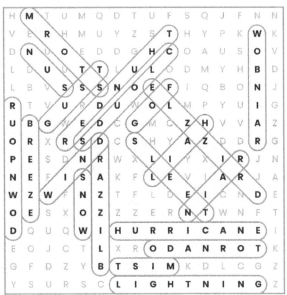

Puzzle #11 - Knots and Ropes - Solution

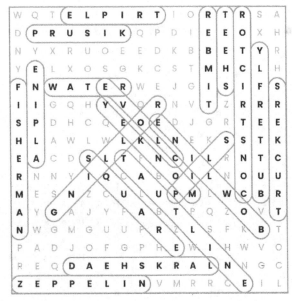

Puzzle #12 - Wildflowers - Solution

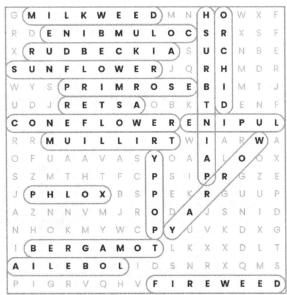

WOODLAND ANIMALS

FOREST FLORA

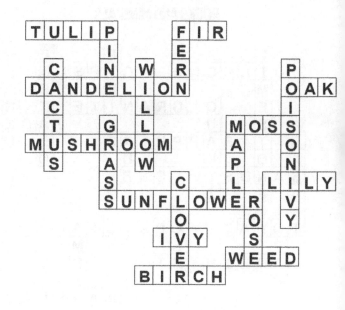

CAMPING ESSENTIALS

WILD WEATHER

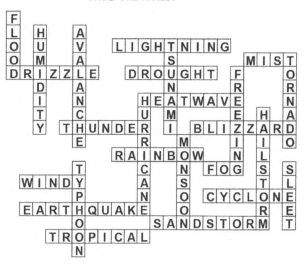

STARS & CONSTELLATIONS

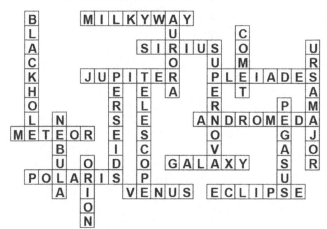

BIRDS OF A FEATHER

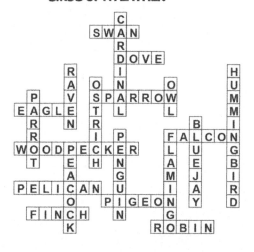

ROCKS AND MINERALS

WHAT'S BUGGING YOU?

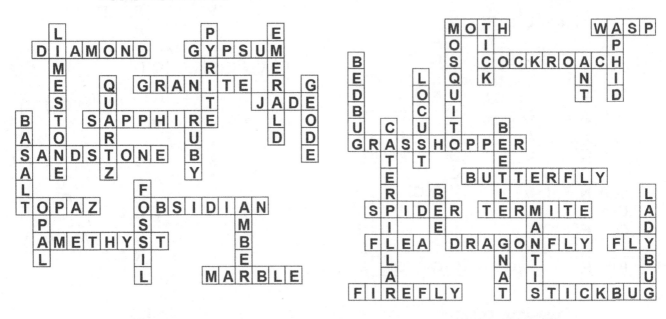

TRIVIA ANSWERS

1. B	19. C	37. A
2. B	20. C	38. C
3. C	21. A	39. B
4. A	22. A	40. A
5. A	23. B	41. C
6. B	24. A	42. A
7. A	25. C	43. B
8. A	26. A	44. B
9. A	27. C	45. A
10. A	28. B	46. B
11. A	29. B	47. B
12. A	30. B	48. B
13. B	31. C	49. B
14. B	32. A	50. C
15. B	33. B	51. B
16. B	34. A	52. B
17. A	35. B	53. B
18. B	36. A	54. B

MAZE 1

MAZE 2

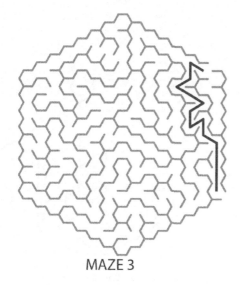

MAZE 3

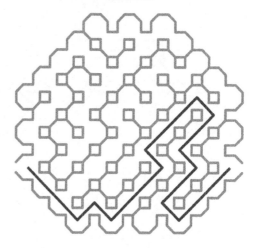

MAZE 4

MAZE 5

MAZE 6

MAZE 7

MAZE 8

MAZE 9

MAZE 10

MAZE 11

MAZE 12

FALLEN PHRASES

1. Bees share information about food sources through an intricate "waggle dance".
2. When threatened, ladybugs secrete a toxic liquid from their leg joints.
3. With a 95% success rate, dragonflies are the world's most effective predators.
4. Fireflies, also known as lightning bugs, are actually bioluminescent beetles, not flies.
5. Praying mantises possess a flexible neck that can turn 180 degrees.
6. Remarkably, cockroaches can survive without their head for one week.
7. Butterflies use their feet to taste, as taste receptors are located there.
8. Rather than sleeping, ants take quick power naps throughout their day.
9. Mosquitoes' wings flap incredibly fast, reaching 500 beats per second.
10. The Western Pygmy Blue is the world's smallest butterfly, just half an inch.
11. Fleas can jump extraordinarily high, up to 200 times their body length.
12. Silkworms create silk, used in textiles, from their salivary glands.
13. Hercules beetles show immense strength, lifting 850 times their own weight.
14. A single termite queen can lay an astounding 30,000 eggs daily.
15. Some cicada species live underground for 17 years before surfacing.
16. The tarantula hawk wasp paralyzes tarantulas to lay eggs inside them.
17. The Bombardier beetle can spray boiling, caustic chemicals when threatened.
18. Adult mayflies live just 24 hours, the shortest lifespan of any insect.
19. Stick insects employ thanatosis, pretending to be dead to evade predators.
20. The giant Atlas moth lacks a mouth, surviving off stored fat from larval stage.⊠

MAD MAP SKILL ANSWERS

1. TENT
2. TREES
3. TENT
4. BACK ON THE STARTING X

CRYPROGRAMS

1 The largest living organism on Earth is not a blue whale or an elephant, but a mushroom! The Armillaria ostoyae covers 2,384 acres

2 Squirrels are incredible climbers and jumpers. They can jump up to 20 feet and can fall from a height of 100 feet without getting hurt.

3 Camping can improve your sleep patterns. Being exposed to natural light during the day helps regulate your body's internal clock.

4 The average hummingbird weighs less than a nickel but has a heart that beats up to 1,260 times per minute.

5 The Appalachian Trail, stretches over 2,190 miles (3,524 kilometers) from Georgia to Maine, passing through fourteen states.

6 Moose are the largest members of the deer family. Their antlers can span up to six feet wide and weigh up to 40 pounds.

7 Trees communicate with each other! Through an underground network of fungi, trees can send chemical signals to warn each other of dangers.

8 The longest recorded hiking trail in the world is the Pacific Crest Trail, which spans over 2,650 miles from Mexico to Canada.

9 Lightning can strike the same place twice, and trees are often the recipients. This is because trees act as natural lightning rods.

10 The Venus flytrap, a carnivorous plant, can close its trap in less than a second when triggered by a bug.

11 A group of owls is called a parliament. These wise birds are known for their exceptional night vision and silent flight.

12 Camping and spending time in nature have been scientifically proven to reduce stress levels and boost mood.

13 The chirping sound of crickets is actually the males singing to attract females. The pattern and speed of their chirps can vary.

14 The Joshua Tree, a unique and iconic plant found in the Mojave Desert, can live for hundreds of years and can to grow up to 40 feet tall.

15 Bald eagles have a wingspan that can reach up to 7 feet. They can also spot a fish from up to a mile away!

16 Pitcher plants have specialized leaves that form a "pitcher" shape, filled with a sticky liquid that traps unsuspecting bugs.

17 The world's largest cave, Son Doong Cave, is so massive that it has its own weather system, complete with clouds and unique ecosystems.

18 A bear can detect scents from up to 20 miles away, making it important to store food properly when camping in bear country.

19 The Great Barrier Reef in Australia is the largest living structure on Earth and is visible from space. It is made up of coral polyps.

20 Fireflies produce light through a process called bioluminescence. They use this light to communicate and attract mates.

Made in the USA
Middletown, DE
28 April 2024

53600868R00071